INTRODUCTION

Andrew's new grill was just waiting to be used.
"I'd grilled many a burger in my day, but now with this new grill, I was ready for the big time. I wanted to try my hand at a grilled swordfish or marinated flank steak. The only problem was I couldn't find a recipe that didn't have a zillion steps or call for some weird ingredient. I thought grilling was supposed to be easy—and fun. I mean, hey, I'm out here in my T-shirt and shorts. Why can't they make it simple?"

Good question. Fortunately, there's **I've got a Grill, Now What?!** It's designed to be simple: All the cooking steps are numbered and all the ingredients are readily available. Better still, all the recipes are delicious. That's because they're from Pam Richards, the fabulous cook who gave you **I'm in the Kitchen, Now What?!** Grilling is her passion, and the recipes here are just unbeatable. Try South Seas Swordfish (page 144) or Asian Flank Steak (page 128) and you'll see what we mean. Yes, grilling is supposed to be fun, easy, and casual. So put on your T-shirt, crank up the grill, and discover for yourself the world's easiest way to cook. Some truly wonderful meals await you.

Barb Chintz
Editorial Director, the *Now What?!*™ series

TABLE OF CONTENTS

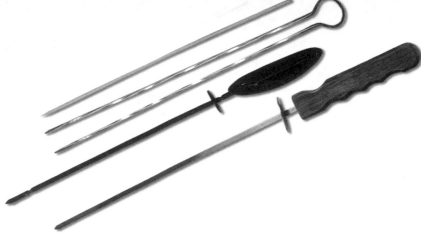

ESSENTIALS OF GRILLING

THE JOYS OF GRILLING

You'll never forget the first time you tasted a grilled tuna steak, fresh off a friend's hibachi—the best fish you'd ever had! But then there were those other occasions when the lamb chops were burned to a crisp or the steak was the consistency of leather. Grilling, you thought, should be left to the talented few.

Think again! **I've got a Grill, Now What?!** shows you how to succeed with everything from pork chops to potatoes, Cornish hens to corn on the cob. The recipes include step-by-step instructions and are written in easy-to-follow language. With a bit of practice, you'll soon see how easy it is to turn out perfectly grilled creations of your own.

Love salmon? Salmon With Mustard Glaze (page 150) requires no marinating and can be ready in less than half an hour, start to finish. Lemon Garlic Chicken Breasts (page 94) are a snap to make, and they'll still draw raves. In addition to seafood and poultry, the chapters cover meats, vegetables, hamburgers, sandwiches, and kebabs—all simple, all delicious.

Yes, you too can grill it yourself—and even star in your own backyard barbecue. The conviviality of friends and neighbors, a tableful of potato salad and baked beans, the smoke wafting from the grill promising good things to come—it's a joyous occasion, as American as a fresh-grilled burger on the Fourth of July.

SAFETY-SMART GRILLING

As fun as it is, grilling also requires some important safety precautions:

Site it right. When setting up your grill, place it on level ground in a well-ventilated area away from anything that could catch fire from floating sparks—including trees and shrubs.

Make sure your grill is scraped clean before you start. Brush or spray the grid with vegetable oil *before* lighting the grill.

Always lift the lid of a gas grill before lighting it. Leaving the lid down can result in a gas buildup and, yes, cause an explosion.

Never leave your grill unattended. It can become very hot, making the grill zone off-limits to children and pets.

Get a fire extinguisher and spray bottle. Make sure you have a fire extinguisher handy—and that you learn how to use it. Failing that, have a box of salt on hand to extinguish grease fires. A spritz of water from a spray bottle will help control flare-ups.

Use lighter fluid properly. If you use lighter fluid with a charcoal grill, make sure to store it far from the fire and from young children. Also, never squirt lighter fluid onto lit coals—the flame can travel up the stream to your hand.

Turn off a gas grill twice. Make sure to shut off a gas grill at the burner as well as at the tank.

Dress smart. Make sure your hair and clothing are grill-safe. Wear grill gloves, tie back long hair, and don't wear loose clothing that could brush up against the firebox. Sandals and open-toe shoes put you at risk for burned toes from dripping grease or falling embers.

CHARCOAL GRILLS

The most common charcoal grill is the bowl-shaped **kettle-style grill**. The glowing coals rest on the bottom grate of the firebox, or "kettle," and a **grill grid** (also called a cooking grid) above the fire holds the food. Many grillers wouldn't dream of using anything but a charcoal grill, touting its advantages over the gas grill: Charcoal burns hotter, it gives food more a "grilled" taste, and it's easy to add wood chunks or herbs to impart a smokier flavor (see page 103). The grills cost from about $30 for a small portable to $450 for a large model with a rolling cart. (For types of charcoal, see page 18.)

Kettle grills should be made of high-grade steel so they won't rust outdoors. The dome, or lid, is often placed on the grill to enhance the grilling process.

An ash catcher at the very bottom of the grill makes it easy to discard the ashes.

Lighting a Charcoal Grill

1. SPREAD lump charcoal or briquettes in a single layer over the charcoal grate of the firebox 1 to 2 inches in diameter wider than the area covered by the food to be cooked. **STACK** the charcoal in a pyramid.

2. BRUSH or spray the grill grid with vegetable oil, or use an oil-dabbed paper towel. (Most recipes require oiling the grid so that food doesn't stick and cleanup is easier.) Set grill grid aside.

3. LIGHT the coals using your choice of starters (see page 15). Once most of the coals have begun to burn, **SPREAD** them in a single layer. Replace cooking grid.

4. When coals are hot enough (see chart below), place food in the center of the grill grid and **GRILL** as directed in the recipe.

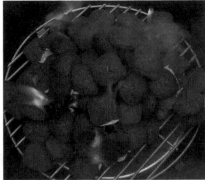

Coals just lighted—fire very hot.

Coals ashen—fire is less intense.

TEMPERATURE	TIME until coals are ready	APPEARANCE
High: 450°–550°F	10–12 minutes	Glows bright orange with virtually no ash
Medium-High: 400°F	12–15 minutes	Glows bright orange with a faint layer of ash (25% ash)
Medium: 325°–350°F	20–25 minutes	Glows orange with a light layer of ash (30% ash)
Medium-Low: 300°F	30–35 minutes	Pale orange with a medium layer of ash (60% ash)
Low: 225°–250°F	40–50 minutes	Faint orange with a thick layer of ash (80–90% ash)

GAS GRILLS

Convenience is the name of the game with gas grills because all you have to do is turn a knob to control the intensity of the flame. A quality gas grill, unlike a charcoal grill, will maintain a consistent temperature for hours. Gas grills are also cleaner to use: Most come with a catch pan built-in under the firebox to catch grease. Propane is the fuel used with most gas grills, and propane cylinder will have to be replaced periodically (see opposite page).

More costly than charcoal grills, gas grills range from $130 for low-end models to a staggering $5,000 for the top of the line. Look for one with at least two burners— or better still, with three or four.

Lighting a Gas Grill

1. BRUSH or spray cooking gride with vegetable oil.

2. With the grill lid open, **TURN** the knob to desired heat. (If the grill doesn't light immediately, check to see if the gas line is open.) **PREHEAT** grill, leaving the lid open. It will take about 15 to 20 minutes for the grill to be hot enough for cooking.

3. ADJUST burners to the temperature specified in the recipe you're using, then **PLACE** food on the grill grid, directly above a burner.

Temperature	Set Burners to
High: 450°–550°F	High
Medium-High: 400°F	Medium High
Medium: 325°–350°F	Medium
Medium-Low: 300°F	Medium Low
Low: 225°–250°F	Low

Changing the Propane Cylinder

Most gas grills come with a gauge that tells you when the propane is getting low. If your grill doesn't have a gauge, you can determine the gas level in one of three ways:

■ Using an attachable gauge, sold at hardware stores.

■ With a bathroom scale: A full cylinder weighs about 38 pounds, a half empty one about 28 pounds, and a dry-as-a-bone tank only about 18 pounds.

■ With an Accu-Level Tape. When boiling water is poured over the tape, which sticks to the side of the cylinder, the tape changes color at gas level. The tape is available where propane-tank supplies are sold.

13

OTHER GRILLS

Electric Grill

Electric grills, used primarily for grilling small pieces of food, free you from having to deal with charcoal, ashes, and propane cylinders—making them ideal for indoor grilling. With most models, the price you pay for such convenience is the absence of the smoky flavor imparted by charcoal.

The best electric grills work like inverted broilers, so foods are at least seared and have the grill marks you get with conventional grills. When choosing an electric grill, make sure it is sturdy and has a thermostatic control. Happily, electric grills aren't very expensive, ranging from $50 to $150.

Hibachi: The Japanese Open grill

The advantage of the hibachi, the smallest of the grills, is portability, which makes it the obvious choice for tailgate parties, the beach, and apartment terraces. The traditional grill of Japan, it has a firebox made of heavy metal that holds in the heat. The firebox is topped by a metal grate, which on many models can be raised or lowered. Vents at the bottom of the firebox allow you to control the heat.

NECESSARY TOOLS

Cleaning Your Grill

Whether you have a gas, charcoal, or electric grill, the grill grid must be clean. The good news is that soap and water aren't required—all you need is a stiff wire brush to scrape off the gunk. For best results use a brass-bristled grill brush (right). The bristles resist rust and won't scratch your grill. If you have a cast-iron grid, buy a brush with steel bristles.

A grill-master tip: After grilling, clean the grid while it is still warm; the heat loosens the food and makes cleaning easier. If you forget, just crank up the grill to heat the grid, then scrape.

Charcoal Starters

A heads-up for charcoal grillers: Get an **electric starter** (left). All you have to do is bury the looped heating element beneath the mound of charcoal, plug in the starter, and the coals will be blazing in 15 minutes.

Another way to start a charcoal fire is with a **chimney starter** (bottom right), an upright aluminum cylinder that's not quite as simple to use but provides a more even fire. Put a crumpled sheet of newspaper in the bottom of the starter, then place it on the bottom grate of the firebox. Put charcoal in the top of the chimney cylinder, and light the newspaper with a match.

Alternatives are **paraffin starters** (small, waxy white cubes) and **sawdust starters** (smaller versions of pressed particle logs). Place either starter under a mound of charcoal and light. Then there's **lighter fluid.** If you use it, be sure to close and remove the can from the vicinity before lighting the charcoal with a match. And *never* spray lighter fluid onto a lit charcoal fire.

BASIC UTENSILS

Here are a few tools of the trade that you'll find indispensable when grilling.

1. Wide metal spatulas with long wooden handles are ideal for flipping burgers, steaks, and chicken pieces.

2. Metal and wooden skewers make turning small foods quick and easy. Wooden skewers should be soaked in water for about 30 minutes before threading with food so that they don't burn. (See page 23 for more on skewers.)

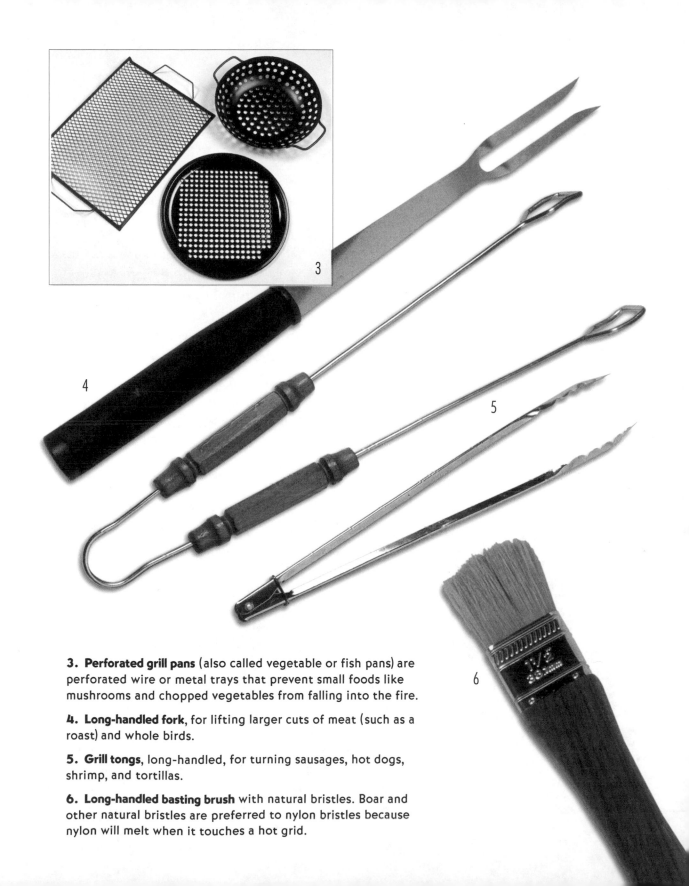

3. Perforated grill pans (also called vegetable or fish pans) are perforated wire or metal trays that prevent small foods like mushrooms and chopped vegetables from falling into the fire.

4. Long-handled fork, for lifting larger cuts of meat (such as a roast) and whole birds.

5. Grill tongs, long-handled, for turning sausages, hot dogs, shrimp, and tortillas.

6. Long-handled basting brush with natural bristles. Boar and other natural bristles are preferred to nylon bristles because nylon will melt when it touches a hot grid.

NOW WHAT DO I DO?

What type of charcoal should I use?

There are three main types of charcoal. **Charwood**, also known as lump charcoal, is made from burned whole logs. This type of charcoal is best because it is pure and burns very hot. **Natural briquettes** are made from pulverized burned wood held together by natural starches. They burn fairly well. **Composition briquettes** are made from burned wood scraps as well as coal dust bound by parafin wax. They do not burn well.

How do I control the heat on a charcoal grill?

You can control the heat in two ways: 1) Adjust the vents on the bottom of the grill. If a recipe calls for closing the lid, close the vents on the top. The more oxygen the coals are exposed to, the hotter they burn—so open the vents for a hotter fire, close them to lower the heat. 2) Or, lower the cooking grid to get more heat, raise it for less.

How often should I clean or replace the catch pan?

Many gas grills have built-in shelves for holding disposable aluminum drip pans. Check the pan for a buildup of food drippings and replace as often as necessary to avoid grease fires. Kettle-style charcoal grills usually come equipped with ash "drip pans," called **ash catchers,** which should be cleaned after each use once the grill has cooled.

Do I have to worry about grilling on windy days?

Grilling on blustery days has its risks. Charcoal grilling provides intense dry heat, but it can be unpredictable—a sudden wind can cause the coals to burn super hot.

How do I keep grease stains off my deck?

Buy a grill mat, also known as a patio protector. Place it underneath your grill to protect your wooden deck or brick patio, not only from stains, but also from sparks and burning embers.

NOW WHERE DO I GO?!

CONTACTS

FOR GRILLS AND GEAR

Weber-Stephen Products Company
800-446-1071
www.weberbbq.com

DeLonghi
800-322-3848
www.delonghiusa.com

Lodge Manufacturing
423-837-7181
www.lodgemfg.com

Char-Broil
800-252-8248
www.charbroil.com

Grilla Gear
800-545-4411
www.grillagear.com

Charcoal Companion
800-521-0505
www.companion-group.com

FOR CHARCOAL AND WOOD

Peoples Woods
800-729-5800
www.peopleswoods.com

W W Wood, Inc.
830-569-2501

BOOKS

Weber's Big Book of Grilling
by Jamie Purviance, Sandra
McCrac, and Tim Turner

**How to Grill: The Complete
Illustrated Book of Barbecue
Techniques**
by Steven Raichien

**George Foreman's Big Book of
Grilling, Barbecue, and Rotisserie**
by George Foreman
and Barbara Witt

**The Best Recipe: Grilling and
Barbecue**
Cook's Illustrated
edited by Carl Tremblay

THINGS ON A STICK

A delicious appetizer that easily can be turned into a main course

SKEWERED BEEF TENDERLOIN

Serves 4–6 ▸▸ Prep Time: 25 minutes ▸▸ Marinating time: 1–4 hours
Grilling Time: 6–8 minutes; medium heat

INGREDIENTS

1/3 cup olive oil

3 tablespoons lemon juice

2 tablespoons mixed dried herbs such as mint, oregano, basil, thyme, rosemary, or sage; or 6 tablespoons mixed fresh herbs

3 cloves garlic, minced

2 tablespoons honey

2 teaspoons Worcestershire sauce

2 pounds beef tenderloin

1 large red bell pepper, seeded and cut into 1-inch pieces

1 large sweet onion, seeded and cut into 1-inch pieces

6 to 8 12-inch metal skewers (see next page)

1. To make the marinade, **WHISK** together in a small bowl the olive oil, lemon juice, mixed herbs, garlic, honey, and Worcestershire sauce.

2. CUT the beef into 1½-inch cubes and place in a large resealable plastic bag.

3. POUR marinade into bag with beef, pressing out the air, and seal; turn bag over several times to coat. **MARINATE** in the refrigerator for at least 1 hour and up to 4 hours, **TURNING** the bag once or twice.

4. REMOVE beef from the bag and discard the marinade.

5. Alternately **THREAD** the beef, bell pepper, and onion pieces onto metal skewers.

6. PREHEAT grill to medium-high.

7. GRILL beef with the grill lid up, 3 to 4 minutes on each side or to desired doneness. Using an oven mitt, **REMOVE** from grill. Use tongs to **PULL** the meat and vegetables off the skewers. **SERVE** immediately.

About Skewers

You can use either metal or bamboo skewers for the recipes in this chapter. **Metal skewers** are somewhat sturdier, but **bamboo skewers** are convenient because, like paper plates, they can be thrown away after use.

Both kinds of skewers come in a variety of lengths and styles. The most common are about 12 inches long, and they are available at most grocery stores. While shorter skewers are occasionally called for, most of the recipes in this chapter require 12-inch skewers.

If you decide to use bamboo skewers, soak them in warm water for at least 30 minutes before using, then allow them to dry. (This will prevent them from burning while the kebabs cook.) Small

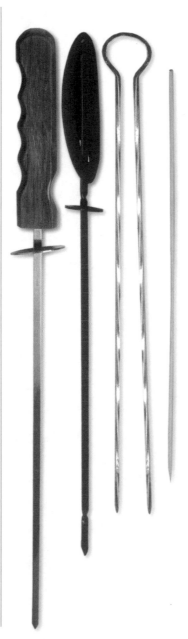

bamboo skewers lend themselves nicely to kebabs with only one or two pieces—usually the case with an hors d'oeuvre or appetizer.

If you opt for metal skewers, be aware that they will be hot to the touch after grilling. Use mitts when removing them from the grill and when removing the food from them.

You can also purchase **two-pronged** metal skewers, which are great for things like shrimp because they keep food from twisting during grilling. If you can't find two-pronged skewers, double-skewer an item simply by using two skewers.

Regardless of which skewers you choose, be careful not to crowd food on them, since bunched-up food won't cook evenly.

Steak fish like tuna and swordfish can stand up to strong flavors and seasonings and won't fall apart while it cooks

GRILLED TUNA BROCHETTES

Serves 6 ↔ Prep Time: 15 minutes ↔ Grilling Time: 4–6 minutes; medium-high heat

INGREDIENTS

2 pounds tuna steaks, cut into 1¼-inch cubes

1 16-ounce can pineapple chunks in juice, drained

3 tablespoons olive oil

1 clove garlic, minced

¼ cup orange juice

1 teaspoon crushed, dried rosemary leaves or **1** tablespoon chopped fresh rosemary leaves

¼ teaspoon each salt and pepper

6 12-inch skewers (see page 23)

1. Using a sharp knife, **CUT** tuna into cubes and place in a large bowl with the pineapple.

2. In a small jar fitted with a lid, **COMBINE** the oil, garlic, orange juice, rosemary, salt, and pepper. **SHAKE** well to mix.

3. POUR over tuna and pineapple, then **TOSS** to coat.

4. Alternately **THREAD** tuna and pineapple onto skewers, being careful not to crowd them. **BRUSH** the kebabs with any remaining orange juice mixture.

5. PREHEAT grill to medium-high.

6. GRILL the kebabs with the grill lid down for about 2 minutes on each side or to desired doneness.

7. Using an oven mitt, **REMOVE** kebabs from grill. **PULL** the tuna and vegetables off the skewer with tongs, then **SERVE** immediately.

FIRST PERSON DISASTER

Grilled Skewers

My roommate and I decided to have a barbecue. We both were tired of the same old chicken, steak, and fish on the grill, so we opted for shish kebabs. We wanted to keep things really simple—paper plates and plastic knives and forks. Disposable bamboo skewers seemed like just the thing, although neither of us had ever used them before.

We marinated everything from lamb to swordfish to vegetables and were proud of our display. By the time our guests arrived, all of the prep work was done, so we could relax and enjoy ourselves. When it was time to eat, we prepared the grill and lined up our skewered creations in the order for grilling. I placed the skewers on the grill and lowered the lid.

When I opened the grill to turn the skewers, I saw that most of them were completely charred—some were even on fire! A friend saw what was happening and asked me if I had soaked the skewers in water beforehand. "That's what keeps them from burning," she said. Live and learn. We wrapped the charred skewer ends in foil and finished grilling.

Amy Z., Madison, Wisconsin

Buying Tuna

Fresh tuna is a tender, firm-textured, rich-flavored fish. When shopping for fresh tuna, look for good color with no browning; a firm, not mushy, feel; and a fresh odor. Ask the fishmonger for the freshest tuna possible, then tell him how you'll be preparing it so that he understands what your recipe requires.

CHICKEN-ZUCCHINI KEBABS

Serves 6 ➥ Prep Time: 20 minutes ➥ Marinating time: 1–2 hours
Grilling Time: 6–8 minutes; medium-high heat

INGREDIENTS

1/2 cup olive oil

1/3 cup dry white wine

3 tablespoons balsamic vinegar

2 teaspoons dried thyme or 2 tablespoons chopped fresh thyme

3 cloves garlic, minced

1/2 teaspoon each salt and pepper

2 pounds boneless, skinless chicken breasts, cut into 1-inch chunks

2 medium zucchinis, trimmed and cut into 1-inch rounds

2 dozen large cherry or grape tomatoes

12 12-inch skewers (see page 23)

1. PLACE the olive oil, wine, vinegar, thyme, garlic, salt, and pepper in a small jar fitted with a lid and shake well. Reserve.

2. RINSE chicken in cold water and pat dry with paper towels.

3. PLACE chicken chunks, zucchini, and tomatoes in a resealable plastic bag, then **POUR** in the marinade.

4. SEAL bag tightly, pressing out the air, and turn over several times to coat ingredients. **MARINATE** in the refrigerator for up to 2 hours. **TURN** bag once or twice during marination.

5. REMOVE the marinated chicken and vegetables from the bag, discarding the marinade.

6. Alternately **THREAD** the chicken, zucchini, and tomatoes onto skewers.

7. PREHEAT grill to medium-high.

8. GRILL the kebabs with the grill lid up for about 2 to 3 minutes on each side, or until the vegetables are tender and the juices run clear when the chicken is pierced with the tip of a sharp knife. Wearing an oven mitt, **REMOVE** kebabs from the grill. Use tongs to **PULL** the chicken and vegetables off the skewers. **SERVE** immediately.

In the Middle East, "kebab" is the term for small pieces of meat
or chicken that are threaded onto a stick and grilled over very high heat.
In most recipes, the high heat sears the meat and seals in the flavor, but
some modern recipes require only medium heat.

This is a simplified version of the traditional Indonesian satay

CHICKEN SATAY WITH PEANUT SAUCE

Serves 6 ↔ Prep Time: 15–20 minutes ↔ Marinating Time: 1–2 hours
Grilling Time: 4 minutes; medium-high heat

INGREDIENTS

2 green onions (white and green parts), finely chopped

½ cup ketchup

4 tablespoons lime juice

⅓ cup soy sauce

4 tablespoons brown sugar

1 tablespoon plus 1 teaspoon vegetable oil

½ teaspoon ground ginger or 2 teaspoons grated ginger (see page 29)

2 cloves garlic, minced

⅓ cup water

2 pounds chicken tenderloins or boneless, skinless chicken breasts, cut into ½-inch-wide by 3-inch-long strips

12 12-inch skewers (see page 23)

⅓ cup creamy peanut butter

1. In a small bowl, **WHISK** together the green onions, ketchup, lime juice, soy sauce, brown sugar, oil, ginger, garlic, and water.

2. RINSE chicken under cold water and pat dry with paper towels, then place in a large resealable plastic bag. **POUR** in half the marinade (reserve the rest), seal bag tightly, and turn it to coat the pieces.

3. MARINATE in refrigerator for 1 to 2 hours. Turn bag once or twice.

4. REMOVE chicken from bag and discard marinade.

5. THREAD one chicken strip onto the end of each skewer by piercing the strip at least twice in a weaving motion (see page 37).

6. BRUSH or spray the cooking grid with vegetable oil. **PREHEAT** grill to medium-high.

7. GRILL chicken with the lid up for 2 minutes on each side, or until the juices run clear when the chicken is pierced with the tip of a sharp knife.

8. BOIL the reserved marinade over medium-high heat for 2 minutes. **ADD** the peanut butter, stirring to combine. **WHISK** until sauce thickens slightly, then remove from heat. Transfer to a small bowl and **SERVE** as a dipping sauce with the satays.

Fresh Ginger

The knobby ginger root can be found in the produce section of most supermarkets. Purchase only smooth, aromatic ginger; if the skin is cracked or wrinkled, the root has seen better days. Use a vegetable peeler to remove the thin, brown skin—but be sure not to peel too deeply, since the delicate flesh just underneath the surface is the most flavorful. Fresh ginger is easily grated with a box grater, or you can peel it and then mince it in a food processor.

Preparing Chicken Tenderloins

The tenderloin is the long, slender muscle found on the inside of the chicken breast. Chicken tenderloins (also called tenders) make great satays. Or, if you want, you can use thin slices of boneless, skinless chicken breasts.

To prepare chicken tenderloins, remove the sinewy tendon found at one end (it is easy to locate because of its white color). Place the tenderloin on a cutting board with the tendon facing downward, then slide a small, sharp paring knife along the tendon, keeping the blade of the knife parallel with the board. Grip the tendon firmly, and pull it off the tenderloin. If you prefer, you can purchase packaged tenderloins at most supermarkets.

Direct and Indirect Grilling

Direct grilling means cooking food on a cooking grid directly over hot coals or, in the case of a gas grill, directly over a flame. Done with the grill lid up sometimes, down other times, it's the preferred method for small, thin pieces of meat like steaks, chicken breasts, fish fillets, and vegetables.

Indirect grilling is similar to roasting. Charcoal is set—or gas burners lit—on each side of the food, not directly beneath it. This method is more suitable for ribs, roasts, whole chickens, turkeys, and other large cuts of meat.

This is a wonderful starter or light main course. Line a table with newspaper and dig in!

GRILLED SHRIMP WITH PINEAPPLE GLAZE

Serves 6 ◆◆ Prep Time: 15 minutes ◆◆ Marinating Time: 15–30 minutes
Grilling Time: 4–6 minutes; high heat

INGREDIENTS

30 large shrimp, deveined (see opposite page), with shells left on

1 16-ounce can crushed pineapple, with juice

2⁄3 cup maple syrup

2⁄3 cup lemon juice

1⁄4 cup Dijon-style mustard

2 tablespoons soy sauce

1⁄4 cup dark rum

6 12-inch metal skewers

I. DEVEIN the shrimp, or buy them already deveined. **RINSE** with water and pat dry with paper towels.

2. MIX the crushed pineapple with juice, maple syrup, lemon juice, mustard, soy sauce, and rum in a medium bowl, then **STIR** to blend.

3. ADD shrimp to the bowl and toss to coat. Set shrimp aside and let **MARINATE** for at least 15 minutes.

4. SKEWER shrimp by first piercing through the head end and then through the tail section. Shrimp should be lying flat.

5. TRANSFER skewers to a platter and **BRUSH** with any remaining marinade.

6. PREHEAT grill to high.

7. GRILL shrimp with the grill lid up for 2 to 3 minutes on each side or until they turn pink. Using an oven mitt, **REMOVE** kebabs from grill. Use tongs to **PULL** shrimp off the skewers. **SERVE** immediately.

The easiest way to devein shrimp to be grilled shell-on
is to use kitchen scissors. Simply cut down the rounded back
of the shrimp and remove the vein with your fingers. If you don't have sharp
kitchen scissors, use a small, sharp paring knife. Easier still
(but slightly more expensive), you can purchase already deveined shrimp in
the fish section of most supermarkets.

Heady rosemary makes this dish absolutely scrumptious! The lamb needs to marinate for several hours, so plan accordingly

ROSEMARY LAMB KEBABS

Serves 4–6 ➼ Prep Time: 15–20 minutes ➼ Marinating Time: 4–8 hours
Grilling Time: 5–6 minutes; high heat

INGREDIENTS

3/4 cup dry red wine

1/4 cup lemon juice

1/4 cup vegetable oil

1/4 cup Dijon-style mustard

4 cloves garlic, minced

3 teaspoons crushed, dried rosemary leaves; or 3 tablespoons chopped fresh rosemary leaves

1/2 teaspoon each salt and pepper

1 1/2- to 2-pound piece leg of lamb, trimmed of fat and cut into 1-inch chunks

2 dozen cherry tomatoes

6 12- to 15-inch skewers (see page 23)

1. In a small jar fitted with a lid, **COMBINE** the red wine, lemon juice, vegetable oil, mustard, garlic, rosemary, salt, and pepper. Screw the lid on tightly and **SHAKE** well to mix.

2. PLACE the lamb pieces in a large resealable plastic bag. **POUR** in the marinade, then press out the air and seal the bag tightly. **TURN** several times to coat lamb pieces evenly. **MARINATE** in the refrigerator for 4 to 8 hours, turning the bag once or twice.

3. REMOVE the lamb from the bag, discarding the marinade.

4. Alternately **THREAD** the lamb and tomatoes onto skewers, being careful not to crowd them.

5. PREHEAT the grill to high.

6. GRILL kebabs with the grill lid up for 2 to 3 minutes on each side or to desired doneness. Using an oven mitt, **REMOVE** kebabs from grill. Use tongs to **PULL** the lamb and tomatoes off the skewers.

7. SERVE immediately, with couscous (a Middle Eastern food that's a cross between rice and pasta) if desired.

TIPS AND TECHNIQUES

Lemon and Lime Juices

Though fresh is always best when you're cooking with lemon or lime juice, it isn't always the easiest or most economical. Don't hesitate to use bottled, reconstituted lemon or lime juice, which can be found in the produce section of your grocery store.

Rosemary

Because it complements almost any grillable food, rosemary is a common addition to marinades. Dried leaves are available, as are crushed, but most cooks find that fresh rosemary is worth the extra effort. The needlelike leaves' distinctive flavor—reminiscent of pine, with just a hint of lemon—comes to full flower when the leaves are chopped right before using. Just be sure to remove them from the woody stems before chopping.

This healthful veggie combo can be served
on its own or alongside any main dish

VEGETABLE MEDLEY WITH BALSAMIC GLAZE

Serves 4–6 •• Prep Time: 20 minutes •• Marinating Time: 30 minutes
Grilling Time: 6–8 minutes; medium heat

INGREDIENTS

4 large portobello mushrooms (4 to 5 inches in diameter), cleaned, then sliced into four wedges each

2 large red or yellow bell peppers, seeded and cut into 2-inch pieces

2 red onions, cut into 2-inch pieces, layers separated

1 cup olive oil

½ cup balsamic vinegar

2 tablespoons lemon juice

4 cloves garlic, minced

3 teaspoons mixed dried herbs such as basil, thyme, oregano, or dill; or 3 tablespoons chopped fresh mixed herbs

½ teaspoon each salt and pepper

4 12- to 15-inch skewers (see page 23)

1. PLACE the portobello mushrooms, bell peppers, and onions in a large bowl.

2. In a small jar fitted with a lid, **COMBINE** the olive oil, vinegar, lemon juice, garlic, herbs, salt, and pepper. Screw the lid on tightly and **SHAKE** well.

3. POUR marinade over vegetables, toss to coat, and let the vegetables **MARINATE** for 30 minutes.

4. PREHEAT grill to medium.

5. Alternately **THREAD** vegetables onto skewers, and **GRILL** with the grill lid up for 6 to 8 minutes, turning vegetables frequently until they are charred and slightly tender. **BRUSH** remaining marinade over vegetables as they grill.

6. Using an oven mitt, **REMOVE** kebabs from grill. Use tongs to **PULL** the vegetables off the skewers. **SERVE** immediately.

TIPS AND TECHNIQUES

Cleaning Mushrooms

Never immerse mushrooms in water, since they act like sponges and absorb liquid very quickly. The best way to clean them is with a mushroom brush, which you can purchase at most grocery stores and any kitchen-supply store.

As an alternative, wipe mushrooms with a damp paper towel. If the mushrooms are covered with a lot of debris, place them in a colander, rinse quickly under cold water. Then immediately pat dry with paper towels.

Fresh vs. Dried Herbs

Virtually all fresh herbs have a dried equivalent. What's the difference? Dried herbs are stronger in flavor, which is why you use less of them in recipes (1 teaspoon of a dried herb is the equivalent of 1 tablespoon of a chopped fresh herb). But does stronger mean better? In a word, no. Fresh herbs enhance the flavor of food with a subtlety that dried herbs can rarely match.

Lime and honey combine to make a tangy marinade that tenderizes flank steak

FLANK STEAK KEBABS

Serves 6 as an appetizer, 4 as a light main course ➼ Prep Time: 15 minutes
Marinating Time: 30 minutes ➼ Grilling Time: 2–4 minutes; medium-high heat

INGREDIENTS

1 bunch scallions (white and green parts), trimmed and minced

1 tablespoon ground ginger or 3 tablespoons minced fresh ginger (see page 29)

3 cloves garlic, minced

3/4 cup soy sauce

1/4 cup red wine

1/3 cup lime juice

4 tablespoons honey

1/2 teaspoon each salt and pepper

1/4 cup vegetable oil

1 flank steak, about 1 1/4 pounds (see page 129), rimmed and cut into 5-inch-long by 1-inch-wide strips

20 12-inch skewers (see page 23)

1. In a medium mixing bowl, **COMBINE** scallions, ginger, garlic, soy sauce, red wine, lime juice, honey, salt, pepper, and oil. **BLEND** until well mixed.

2. WEAVE flank steak slices onto the skewers.

3. ARRANGE skewers in a shallow dish and **POUR** marinade over them. **MARINATE** at room temperature for 30 minutes, turning skewers once or twice in the marinade during that time.

4. BRUSH the grill grid with oil. **PREHEAT** to medium-high.

5. GRILL beef with the grill lid up for about 1 to 2 minutes per side or to desired doneness. **TRANSFER** to a platter and **SERVE** immediately. (If using metal skewers, remove meat from skewers before serving.)

To weave strips of flank steak or any other meat onto a skewer, pinch a 1 1/2- to 2-inch section of meat between your thumb and forefinger and pierce with the skewer. Flatten the meat on the skewer and repeat until it is well-secured.

37

This is an updated version of the classic lamb shish kebab

SKEWERED LAMB WITH EGGPLANT AND TOMATOES

Serves 6 ➥ Prep Time: 30 minutes ➥ Marinating Time: 1 hour
Grilling Time: 12–15 minutes; high heat

INGREDIENTS

1/3 cup olive oil

2 tablespoons red wine vinegar

2 tablespoons dry sherry

2 teaspoons crushed, dried rosemary leaves or 2 tablespoons chopped fresh rosemary

3 cloves garlic, minced

1 teaspoon each salt and pepper

2 pounds boneless leg of lamb, cut in 2-inch cubes

1 large eggplant cut in 2-inch chunks; or 3 baby eggplants, cut into quarters (see page 91)

3 large plum tomatoes, cut in half lengthwise

6 12-inch skewers (see page 23)

1. In a large bowl, **COMBINE** the oil, vinegar, sherry, rosemary, garlic, salt, and pepper. **RESERVE** 1/4 cup marinade for basting.

2. ADD the lamb, eggplant, and tomatoes to the bowl and toss to coat with the marinade. **MARINATE** at room temperature for 1 hour, tossing once or twice during marination.

3. BRUSH grill grid with vegetable oil. **PREHEAT** grill to high.

4. Alternately **THREAD** skewers with the lamb and vegetables. **BRUSH** the skewered food with the reserved marinade and place the skewers on the grill.

5. GRILL with the grill lid up, 5 to 7 minutes on each side. Baste frequently with reserved marinade (see opposite page), up to within 5 minutes of doneness, or until the lamb is cooked to desired doneness and vegetables are tender.

6. Wearing an oven mitt, **REMOVE** kebabs from grill. Use tongs to **PULL** the lamb, eggplant, and tomatoes off the skewers. **SERVE** immediately.

Marinades in a Jar

What could be simpler than putting all of your sauce or marinade ingredients in a jar, closing the lid, and shaking? Just be sure to screw the lid on tightly.

Basting

To baste means to pour, brush, or drizzle a liquid over whatever you're cooking (or grilling). The purpose? To moisten and add flavor to food as it cooks.

It's best not to baste with the marinade in which you have been soaking raw meat, fish, or poultry. Use only marinade liquid that has been set aside (reserved).

When grilling fruit, use direct medium heat unless the recipe instructs otherwise. For outstanding results, choose only the ripest fruit

GRILLED FRUIT KEBABS WITH ORANGE GLAZE

Serves 6 ◆◆ Prep Time: 20 minutes ◆◆ Grilling Time: 8 minutes; medium heat

INGREDIENTS

1 cup orange juice

2 tablespoons honey

2 tablespoons lime juice

1 tablespoon orange-flavored liqueur (such as Cointreau)

2 teaspoons cornstarch

1 16-ounce can pineapple chunks in juice, drained, or 2 cups fresh pineapple chunks

18 fresh strawberries, hulled

1 pound cake (store-bought is fine), cut into 1 1/2-inch cubes

6 12- to 15-inch skewers (see page 23)

Vanilla ice cream, optional

I. To make the glaze, **COMBINE** the orange juice, honey, lime juice, liqueur, and cornstarch in a small saucepan and **WHISK** until smooth. **COOK,** stirring, over medium-high heat for 1 to 2 minutes, or until thickened. Set aside.

2. Alternately **THREAD** pineapple, strawberries, and cake on the skewers. **BRUSH** the fruit and cake with the glaze, coating well.

3. PREHEAT the grill to medium.

4. GRILL fruit and cake with the grill lid up, for about 3 minutes on each side or until they start to brown.

5. SERVE fruit skewers with warm glaze and ice cream. (If using metal skewers, remove fruit from skewers before serving.)

TIPS AND TECHNIQUES

Grilling Fruit

Grilling can intensify the flavor of everything from bananas to stone fruits like peaches. When grilling bananas, choose small ones or slice medium to large ones crosswise on the diagonal. To grill Thai-style, dip the bananas in coconut milk, then in a mixture of sugar and cinnamon; shake off any excess. Grill for 2 to 3 minutes on each side. If you want to grill peaches, plums, nectarines, or other stone fruits, peel, cut them in half, and remove the pits before grilling for 5 to 6 minutes on the skinless side only.

Choosing Honey

There are hundreds of types of honey, their varying colors and flavors determined not by the bees but by their nectar source: the flowers of clover, orange blossoms, or myriad wildflowers. Here's a rule of thumb for buying: the darker the honey, the stronger the flavor.

Liquid honey, which is usually pasteurized to prevent crystallization, is the honey to use in recipes. For those who like to eat honey "out of hand," **comb honey** comes in its edible, if chewy, honeycomb. Occupying the middle ground is **chunk-style honey**, so named because it has pieces of honeycomb floating in it.

BURGERS

A hamburger with "the works" is what
grilling is all about!

THE PERFECT BURGER

Serves 6 ↬ Prep Time: 5 minutes ↬ Grilling Time: 10–12 minutes; medium-high heat

INGREDIENTS

2 pounds ground
beef (chuck)

$1/2$ teaspoon each salt and
pepper

Vegetable oil for brushing
grill

6 hamburger buns, split
and toasted (see page 61),
or 1 loaf French bread cut
into 12 $1/2$-inch-thick
slices, toasted

TOPPINGS

Ketchup

Mustard

Salsa

Lettuce leaves

Tomato slices

Sliced red onions

Thin slices of assorted
cheese (Muenster,
American, cheddar,
Monterey Jack)

1. In a medium bowl, **COMBINE** the meat, salt and pepper.

2. SHAPE into six patties, each about $3/4$ of an inch thick, being careful not to overhandle the meat.

3. BRUSH or spray the grill grid with vegetable oil. **PREHEAT** to medium-high.

4. GRILL burgers with the grill up for about 1 minute on each side, then lower the lid and grill for 4 to 5 minutes on each side or until no pink remains. Resist the urge to press down on the burgers, since pressure will release valuable juices.

5. PLACE burgers on buns or the bread of your choice (see page 61), **TOP** with your favorite fixin's, and **SERVE** immediately.

NOTE: If you want to make cheeseburgers, put a slice of cheese on the burger about 3 minutes before the meat is done.

Ask the Experts

What kind of hamburger meat should I buy to make grilled burgers?
That depends on how concerned you are about the fat content of the meat. Not surprisingly, the more fat in the meat, the juicier it will taste. That's because fat acts as a taste enhancer, allowing flavors to linger longer.

The fat in hamburger meat can vary, depending on which cut of meat is used. Ground sirloin (15% fat) is lower in fat than ground round (20% fat). Ground chuck, which contains about 30% fat, will produce the juiciest burgers.

I used ground chuck, but my burgers still came out tough. What happened?
Chances are you committed a common burger-grilling boo-boo: overhandling the meat. When forming hamburger patties, try not to squeeze or roll the meat around too much.

How do I make my burgers moist, especially if I use lean ground sirloin?
Use meat that's coarsely rather than finely ground. And watch how much you handle the meat. The less handling, the moister the burger.

TERIYAKI BEEF BURGERS

Serves 6 ♦ Prep Time: 10–12 minutes ♦ Grilling Time: 10–12 minutes; medium-high heat

INGREDIENTS

3/4 cup plain dried bread-crumbs

1/2 small red onion, chopped

3 tablespoons water

1 tablespoon honey

1 1/2 tablespoons soy sauce

2 cloves garlic, minced

1 teaspoon ground ginger or 1 tablespoon minced fresh ginger (see page 29)

1 1/2 pounds ground beef chuck

6 buns, split and toasted (see page 61)

1. In a large bowl, **STIR** together breadcrumbs, onion, water, honey, soy sauce, garlic, and ginger.

2. MIX the ground beef into the breadcrumb mixture and gently combine, taking care not to overmix.

3. SHAPE the beef into 6 3/4-inch-thick patties.

4. BRUSH or spray grill grid with vegetable oil. **PREHEAT** to medium-high.

5. GRILL burgers with the grill lid down for about 5 to 6 minutes per side or until cooked to desired doneness. **SERVE** burgers on toasted buns.

Homemade Breadcrumbs

No store-bought bread-crumbs on hand? Making breadcrumbs at home is simple: Just tear 2 or 3 slices of toasted bread into small pieces then chop in a blender until crumbled. For the teriyaki burgers, you'll want to use white bread, but you can get creative when adding breadcrumbs to plain burgers: Rye, whole wheat, sourdough, or multi-grain crumbs will add sub-tle flavor to the patties. You could also add a dash of sea-soning to the crumbs—dried thyme, oregano, rosemary, sage, parsley, or any other herb that goes well with meat.

Buying Soy Sauce

A staple of Asian cooking, soy sauce is dark and salty, the product of fermenting boiled soybeans and roasted wheat or barley. When pick-ing a soy sauce from the grocer's shelf, most cooks look only for regular vs. low sodium. But there's another difference as well—light vs. dark. **Light soy sauce** is thinner and saltier than **dark soy sauce**, which is usually darkened with caramel.

This variation of the traditional cheeseburger uses onion and other seasonings, making it all the more delectable

SUMPTUOUS CHEESEBURGERS

Serves 6–8 ⬥ Prep Time: 10 minutes
Grilling Time: 10–12 minutes for medium; medium-high heat

INGREDIENTS

2 pounds ground beef (chuck)

1 small red onion, chopped

2 cloves garlic, minced

2 tablespoons Worcestershire sauce

2 tablespoons dried basil or $\frac{1}{3}$ cup fresh basil, chopped

2 tablespoons Dijon-style mustard

$\frac{1}{2}$ teaspoon each salt and pepper

6 to **8** slices Monterey Jack cheese

6 to **8** buns, split and toasted (see page 61)

1. In a medium bowl, **MIX** the ground beef, onion, garlic, Worcestershire, basil, mustard, salt, and pepper until just combined, being careful not to overhandle the meat (see page 45).

2. SHAPE into 6 to 8 patties about $\frac{1}{2}$- to $\frac{3}{4}$-inch thick. (Refrigerate until ready to use, or proceed with recipe.)

3. BRUSH or spray the grill grid with vegetable oil. **PREHEAT** grill to medium-high.

4. GRILL patties with the grill lid up, 1 minute per side, then lower the lid and grill 4 minutes per side or to desired doneness. During the last minute or two of grilling, **TOP** each burger with a slice of cheese, lower lid and allow the cheese to melt. **GRILL** or toast buns just before serving. **SERVE** each cheeseburger in a toasted bun.

The highly seasoned meat in this cheeseburger
is balanced by mild Monterey Jack cheese.
Burger lovers who want to boost the flavor even more
can opt for a sharp cheddar cheese.

STUFFED BEEF BURGERS

Serves 6 ↣ Prep Time: 15–20 minutes ↣ Refrigeration Time: 1 hour
Grilling Time: 12–16 minutes; medium-high heat

INGREDIENTS

3 ounces goat cheese, softened

4 tablespoons butter, softened

2 cloves garlic, minced

2 teaspoons mixed dried herbs such as parsley, basil, thyme, oregano, chives, or 2 tablespoons fresh herbs, chopped and mixed

2 pounds ground beef (chuck)

1/2 teaspoon each salt and pepper

6 sesame seed hamburger buns, split and toasted (see page 61)

FOR THE GOAT-CHEESE BUTTER

1. COMBINE the goat cheese, butter, garlic, and herbs in a small bowl.

2. SCRAPE butter onto a sheet of plastic wrap and **ROLL** into a log. **REFRIGERATE** for 1 hour. When ready to grill, remove from refrigerator and unwrap.

3. SLICE log into 6 discs.

FOR THE PATTIES

1. In a medium bowl, **COMBINE** beef with salt and pepper and **MIX** until well blended, making sure not to overhandle the meat.

2. SHAPE into 6 balls. Using your thumb, make a depression in the center of each ball and **FILL** with a disc of butter.

3. FOLD the meat over to cover the butter, then form the burgers into round patties about 1-inch thick.

4. BRUSH or spray the grill grid with vegetable oil. **PREHEAT** the grill to medium high.

5. GRILL burgers with the lid down for about 6 to 8 minutes on each side or to desired doneness. **SERVE** the burgers on toasted buns.

TIPS AND TECHNIQUES

Herb Blends

When it comes to seasoning meat patties, you can either invent your own herb blends or turn to one of the classics. **Italian seasoning**, sold at supermarkets, is a mixture of thyme, oregano, marjoram, summer savory, rosemary, basil, and sage. **Fines herbes** is a finely chopped mixture of parsley, chervil, chives, and tarragon. **Herbes de Provence** is a heavenly scented blend of lavender flowers, thyme, marjoram, rosemary, and summer savory. All of these Mediterranean blends can be purchased at supermarkets or gourmet shops.

Ask The Experts

Can I make the goat-cheese butter ahead of time?
This savory goat-cheese butter will keep in the refrigerator for up to a week. It can be made even earlier and kept frozen for several months. And you don't have to save it for just burgers: It's great for topping grilled vegetables, too.

Italian Seasoning

Herbes de Provence

51

These burgers have some healthy mix-ins, but feel free to add whatever your heart desires!

BURGERS WITH A TWIST

Serves 6 ➹ Prep Time: 15 minutes ➹ Grilling Time: 8 minutes; medium-high heat

INGREDIENTS

1 pound ground beef (chuck)

1 10-ounce box frozen chopped spinach, thawed and squeezed dry

½ cup chopped sun-dried tomatoes (packed in oil or dry and refreshed, see next page)

¾ cup canned small white beans (cannellini), rinsed and drained

½ small onion, chopped

1 teaspoon lemon juice

½ teaspoon salt

½ teaspoon pepper

6 buns, split and toasted (see page 61)

1. In a medium bowl, **COMBINE** the ground beef, spinach, sun-dried tomatoes, beans, onion, lemon juice, salt, and pepper. **MIX** until just blended.

2. SHAPE into 6 ½-inch-thick patties.

3. BRUSH or spray the grill grid with vegetable oil. **PREHEAT** grill to medium-high.

4. GRILL burgers with lid up for 4 minutes per side for medium rare. **REMOVE** from grill, **ADD** toppings of your choice (see page 44), and **SERVE** on toasted buns.

Sun-Dried Tomatoes

Sun-dried tomatoes are usually dried in the sun, resulting in a chewy, intensely flavored, sweet, dark-red tomato. You can buy them dry, packed in oil, or in paste form. Dry-packed sun-dried tomatoes are far less expensive than those packed in oil (it's the oil you're paying for!), and the only disadvantage is that they have to be refreshed, or rehydrated, before you use them. To refresh, place them in a bowl, cover with boiling water, and allow to stand for about 15 minutes. Drain, then pat the tomatoes dry with paper towels before using.

The mustard sauce goes well with traditional hamburgers, but it's equally good with pork or any type of poultry

BURGERS WITH MUSTARD SAUCE

Serves 6 ↦ Prep Time: 15 minutes ↦ Grilling Time: 10–12 minutes; medium-high heat

INGREDIENTS

2/3 cup Dijon-style mustard

1/2 cup mayonnaise

1/2 cup reduced-fat sour cream

3 teaspoons Worcestershire sauce

1 clove garlic, minced

2 pounds ground beef (preferably chuck)

1 teaspoon each salt and pepper

6 buns, split and toasted (see page 61)

1. In a small bowl, **WHISK** together the mustard, mayonnaise, sour cream, Worcestershire sauce, and garlic. (If making ahead, cover the sauce with plastic wrap; it will keep in the refrigerator for up to 5 days.)

2. In a medium bowl, **COMBINE** the beef, salt, and pepper.

3. SHAPE mixture into 6 1/2-inch-thick patties.

4. BRUSH or spray the grill grid with vegetable oil. **PREHEAT** grill to medium-high.

5. GRILL burgers with the lid down for 5 to 6 minutes per side for medium. **REMOVE** burgers from the grill and place on on toasted buns. **SPOON** mustard sauce over the meat and **SERVE** immediately.

Beyond Dijon

You can use other mustards besides Dijon when making mustard sauce, but give it some thought. The French Dijon is spicier than most American mustards, but not as hot as the fiery preparations of the Chinese. German prepared mustards range from very hot to sweet and mild. And what about that American favorite, bright-yellow "ballpark" mustard? As much as it's loved, it's better used on hot dogs than in sauces.

Meat Blends for Burgers

For variety and extra flavor, make hamburger patties with half ground chuck and half ground pork. Or pair the pork with ground veal. Beef-and-pork burgers are less dense than all-beef burgers. Veal-and-pork burgers have even less fat but a milder taste; they will benefit from the addition of an herb blend (see page 51).

LAMB BURGERS IN PITA WITH YOGURT SAUCE

Serves 4 ◆◆ Prep Time: 20 minutes ◆◆ Grilling Time: 10 minutes; medium-high heat

INGREDIENTS

1 cup plain yogurt

1 teaspoon ground ginger

2 teaspoons dried mint; or 2 tablespoons chopped fresh mint

1½ pounds lean ground lamb

1 tablespoon dried basil; or ¼ cup chopped fresh basil

1 tablespoon dried parsley

2 tablespoons lemon juice

2 cloves garlic, minced

½ teaspoon ground cumin

1 teaspoon salt

½ teaspoon pepper

4 pita-bread rounds

FOR THE SAUCE (MAKE AHEAD)

1. COMBINE the yogurt, ginger, and mint in a small bowl.

2. REFRIGERATE, then allow sauce to return to room temperature before using.

FOR THE BURGERS

1. In a medium bowl, **MIX** lamb, basil, parsley, lemon juice, garlic, cumin, salt, and pepper.

2. SHAPE into 4 patties about ¾-inch thick.

3. BRUSH or spray the grill grid with vegetable oil. **PREHEAT** grill to medium-high.

4. GRILL burgers with lid down for about 5 minutes on each side or until browned on the outside and no longer pink in the middle.

5. SERVE in pita bread and **TOP** with yogurt sauce.

The minty yogurt sauce on
these Middle Eastern–style
burgers provides a cooling
contrast to the spiced lamb.

A healthy hamburger with a kick

SIMPLE TURKEY BURGERS

Serves 6 ➻ Prep Time: 10 minutes ➻ Grilling Time: 10 minutes; medium-high heat

INGREDIENTS

2 pounds lean ground turkey

4 green onions (white and green parts), chopped

2 cloves garlic, minced

$^1/_2$ tablespoon Worcestershire sauce

$^1/_4$ teaspoon cayenne pepper

Salt and pepper to taste

Sliced cheese, optional

6 buns split and toasted (see page 61) or 6 French bread slices

1. In a medium bowl, **COMBINE** turkey, green onions, garlic, Worcestershire, cayenne, salt, and pepper. **MIX** thoroughly.

2. SHAPE mixture into 6 1-inch-thick patties.

3. BRUSH or spray the grill grid with vegetable oil. **PREHEAT** grill to medium-high.

4. GRILL burgers with lid up for 5 minutes per side or until no pink remains. **TOP** burgers with a slice of cheese during the last minute of grilling, if desired. **SERVE** on toasted buns or French bread.

The Case for Turkey

Compared to other burger meats, just how healthful is turkey? The answer is in the percentages. Ground skinless turkey breast gets only 5% of its calories from fat, compared to 77% for ground beef. It's important to note that these figures are for *skinless* turkey; turkey ground with the skin on gets almost 10 times the calories from fat.

Another tip: Frozen ground turkey may not hold together in a patty as well as fresh ground turkey, so keep that in mind when you shop.

Burgers of a Different Stripe

Buffalo burgers aren't just some Western curiosity. Some 2000 producers raise bison for meat in the United States to provide for a growing market. It is sporadically available in butcher shops. Buffalo meat is lower in fat and cholesterol than most cuts of beef and has more iron. (Because the meat is so lean, you should cook it slowly over low heat.)

A delicious combination of flavors, equally good with ground chicken

SOUTHWEST TURKEY BURGERS

Serves 6 ➡ Prep Time: 15 minutes ➡ Grilling Time: 10 minutes; medium-high heat

INGREDIENTS

1/4 cup Worcestershire sauce

1/4 cup ketchup

1 tablespoon soy sauce

1 teaspoon chili powder

1/4 teaspoon ground cumin

2 pounds lean ground turkey

3 cloves garlic, minced

1 small onion, chopped

1/4 cup dried bread-crumbs

6 buns, split and toasted (see next page)

Lettuce and sliced tomatoes, optional

1. COMBINE Worcestershire sauce, ketchup, soy sauce, chili powder, and cumin in a small bowl. Set aside.

2. In a medium bowl, gently **COMBINE** turkey, garlic, onion, breadcrumbs, and 1/4 cup of sauce.

3. SHAPE turkey mixture into 6 3/4-inch-thick patties and **BRUSH** both sides with additional sauce.

4. BRUSH or spray the grill grid with vegetable oil. **PREHEAT** grill to medium-high.

5. GRILL burgers with lid up for 5 minutes per side or until no pink remains.

6. TOAST buns on grill for 1 minute. **SERVE** burgers on buns with lettuce and slices of tomato, if desired.

TIPS AND TECHNIQUES

Breads for Burgers

When you get that craving for a hamburger, only a traditional bun will do. But that doesn't mean you can't occasionally branch out and try other breads. Just make sure the bread isn't so soft or crumbly that it comes apart while you eat. Good choices are English muffins and slices of dense French, Italian, rye, sourdough, and whole-grain breads.

Toasting Buns

Whether to toast burger buns is a matter of personal choice, but most people find that toasting provides that magical finishing touch.

To toast buns (or any other bread used for a hamburger), wait until your burgers are just about done, then place the buns face down directly on the grill or a perforated grill pan. Check them after 30 seconds, since they can burn quickly.

If you'd rather take a slower approach, place a sheet of foil underneath the buns and heat for 5 minutes. Check the buns frequently.

These are a snap to prepare and are great
served on toasted English muffins

TURKEY BURGERS WITH DILL

Serves 6 ↦ Prep Time: 10 minutes ↦ Grilling Time: 10 minutes; medium-high heat

See page 61

INGREDIENTS

1½ pounds lean ground turkey

¾ cup mayonnaise

¼ cup chopped red onion

1 tablespoon dried dill; or 3 tablespoons chopped fresh dill

2 tablespoons drained capers or pickle relish

2 tablespoons Worcestershire sauce

Salt and pepper to taste

Olive oil for brushing muffins

6 toasted English muffins or burger buns, split and toasted (see page 61)

1. In a large bowl, gently **COMBINE** turkey, mayonnaise, onion, dill, capers, Worcestershire sauce, salt, and pepper.

2. SHAPE into 6 ¾-inch-thick patties.

3. BRUSH or spray the grill grid with vegetable oil. **PREHEAT** grill to medium-high.

4. GRILL burgers with lid up for 5 minutes per side or until no pink remains. **BRUSH** the English muffins lightly with olive oil and **GRILL** for 1 minute, cut-side down. Assemble the burgers and **SERVE** immediately.

What Are Capers?

The culinary use of the pickled flower buds called capers dates back to ancient Greece and Rome. Today, the piquant buds of the Mediterranean shrub *Capparis spinosa* lend flavor to sauces and condiments and are used as a garnish for meat and vegetable dishes.

Olive green in color, capers range in size from the Provençal nonpareil variety (about ¼ inch in diameter and considered the finest) to Italian capers, about twice the size of the nonpareils.

If these little delicacies seem on the expensive side, it's because harvesting them is labor-intensive: The buds develop so quickly, they have to be picked almost daily, then sun-dried before being pickled in a vinegar brine.

A Dill Look-alike

In appearance, feathery fennel leaves are almost indistinguishable from fresh dill. In fact, food shoppers often confuse the two. While fennel's flavor gave rise to one of its common names, sweet anise, the moniker is somewhat misleading. The leaves are less licoricey than anise, and their taste becomes more delicate still when they are cooked.

These are delicious and healthful—and just as good when made with ground chicken

TURKEY BURGERS WITH FETA CHEESE

Serves 6 ❧ Prep Time: 10 minutes ❧ Grilling Time: 8–10 minutes; medium-high heat

INGREDIENTS

2 pounds lean ground turkey

1 large egg white, lightly beaten

½ small red onion, chopped

4 ounces crumbled feta cheese

1 teaspoon dried thyme

½ teaspoon each salt and pepper

6 sesame seed hamburger buns, split open and toasted (see page 61)

1. In a medium bowl, **COMBINE** the turkey, egg white, onion, feta cheese, thyme, salt, and pepper.

2. MIX gently until all the ingredients are blended, taking care not to overhandle the meat.

3. SHAPE mixture into 6 patties, about 3/4-inch thick.

4. BRUSH or spray the grill grid with vegetable oil. **PREHEAT** grill to medium-high.

5. GRILL burgers with grill lid down for about 4 to 5 minutes per side or until golden brown and cooked through with no pink remaining. **SERVE** on toasted buns.

Feta Cheese

Feta is sometimes referred to as "pickled cheese" because it is cured and stored in its own whey brine. The best known cheese of Greece, it was traditionally made with goat's or sheep's milk; today, many commercial fetas are made from cow's milk. Chalky white, rindless, and crumbly, the cheese has a flavor that adds tang and richness to salads and cooked dishes.

Other Cheese Choices

Crumbly cheeses like feta are good for mixing with burger meat, so let your taste buds be your guide. Blue cheeses, including Roquefort, add pungency, while English cheeses like Caerphilly and Wensley-dale (both available in food stores with a serious cheese section) are flavorful but mild.

FIRST PERSON DISASTER

Where's the Cheese?

There's nothing quite like a plump, juicy cheeseburger cooked over charcoal. One day my husband was tending to the fire, and after flipping the burgers, he topped each with a good helping of cheese. He closed the lid and went inside the house to get the buns.

By the time he got back, half the cheese had fallen off the burgers and was now glued to the grill rack. I guess a minute away from the grill when waiting for cheese to melt isn't such a good idea after all. To top it off, it took a lot of elbow grease to get that cheese off the grill grid!

Carol G., Corsicana, Texas

These burgers are succulent and a welcome change from the standard turkey burger

GOAT CHEESE-STUFFED TURKEY BURGERS

Serves 6 ↦ Prep Time: 15 minutes ↦ Grilling Time: 8–10 minutes; high heat

INGREDIENTS

1½ pounds lean ground turkey

6 tablespoons dried breadcrumbs

3 tablespoons lemon juice

1 tablespoon dried thyme

¼ cup chopped red onion

1 teaspoon salt

¼ teaspoon pepper

8 ounces goat cheese, sliced into 6 ½-inch rounds

6 buns, split and toasted (see page 61)

Lettuce and sliced tomato or bell peppers, optional

1. In a medium bowl, **COMBINE** the turkey, breadcrumbs, lemon juice, thyme, onion, salt, and pepper.

2. DIVIDE mixture into 6 equal portions, then divide each portion in half. **SHAPE** each half into ½-inch-thick patties. There should be 12 patties in all.

3. PLACE one round of goat cheese on top of each of 6 patties, then sandwich together with another patty. **PINCH** top and bottom of patties together to seal in cheese.

4. BRUSH or spray the grill grid with vegetable oil. **PREHEAT** grill to high.

5. GRILL burgers with lid up for 4 to 5 minutes per side or until no pink remains. **TOP** burgers with lettuce and tomato or bell pepper slices. **SERVE** on toasted buns.

Soft Cheeses

France is home to many of the best goat's-milk cheeses (*chèvres*), with Bucheron perhaps the best-known brand. But not all soft cheeses are made from goat's milk. Brie and Camembert, for example, are made from cow's milk. Stronger in flavor, both make a good substitute for goat cheese in the recipe on the opposite page. For each burger, just scoop out a couple of tablespoons from a wedge of either cheese (no rind, please), then proceed as directed.

Herbal Enhancements

To give extra flavor to grilled foods, add herbs to the hot coals, a few sprigs at a time. Thyme, rosemary, oregano, and sage are popular choices. Before tossing herbs onto the coals, soak the sprigs in water and shake off the excess.

Other flavor enhancers are dry grapevine cuttings, which add a sweet, slightly winelike flavor to grilled foods; they work best with fish and poultry. When you toss the grapevine cuttings onto the fire, they'll produce a quick burst of heat before lightly smoking. (For adding wood to charcoal, see page 103.)

These burgers are good served open-faced on French bread. Add a green salad to this entrée, and you have the perfect lunch menu

CRAB BURGERS

Serves 6 ◆ Prep Time: 15–20 minutes ◆ Grilling Time: 8 minutes; medium-high heat

INGREDIENTS

3 6-ounce cans lump crabmeat, drained and picked through (see opposite page)

3 cups dry white bread-crumbs, divided

2 bunches green onions (white and green parts), chopped

¾ cup mayonnaise, divided

1 tablespoon seafood seasoning, such as Old Bay

2 large egg whites, lightly beaten

½ teaspoon salt

1 teaspoon pepper

4 tablespoons Dijon-style mustard

Vegetable oil

6 slices French bread

1. In a medium bowl, **COMBINE** crabmeat, 2 cups of the bread-crumbs, green onions, ½ cup of mayonnaise, seafood seasoning, egg whites, salt, and pepper.

2. SHAPE mixture into 6 patties.

3. PLACE the remaining breadcrumbs on a plate and **COAT** the patties with them, turning to coat completely.

4. BLEND the remaining mayonnaise and the Dijon mustard in a small bowl, then **REFRIGERATE** until ready to use.

5. BRUSH or spray the grill grid with vegetable oil. **PREHEAT** grill to medium-high.

6. GRILL burgers with lid down for about 4 minutes on each side or until golden brown. **TOAST** bread slices for 1 minute per side or until lightly browned. **SPREAD** mustard-mayonnaise sauce on bread and top with patties. **SERVE** immediately.

TIPS AND TECHNIQUES

Prepared Crabmeat

This recipe calls for canned crabmeat, but prepackaged crab also comes frozen and pasteurized. Pasteurized crab is heated in cans at a temperature high enough to kill bacteria, but not as high as that used for regular canning. Whatever you choose, be aware that even prepackaged crabmeat warrants a close inspection for stray bits of shell. Look for thcm by picking through the meat with a fork.

Buying Fresh

Fresh crabmeat, usually sold by the pound and ready to use, can be found in the seafood section of most supermarkets or at your local fish market.

Lump crabmeat is whole pieces of the white body meat, while **flaked crabmeat** includes small pieces of light and dark meat from the body and claws.

For a delicious change from grilled tuna steaks, try tuna burgers

GRILLED TUNA BURGERS

Serves 6 ↔ Prep Time: 20 minutes ↔ Grilling Time: 8 minutes; medium-high heat

INGREDIENTS

2 pounds tuna steaks, coarsely chopped

1/3 cup plain dry bread-crumbs, divided

1 cup mayonnaise, divided

1/2 cup finely chopped cornichons or other mild pickles

2 teaspoons dried dill weed or 2 tablespoons finely chopped fresh dill

1 tablespoon lemon juice

1/4 teaspoon salt

1/2 teaspoon pepper

2 tablespoons Dijon-style mustard

2 beefsteak tomatoes, cut in 1/2-inch-thick slices

I. Using a large, sharp knife, **CHOP** the tuna by hand until it resembles chopped meat.

2. In a medium bowl, **COMBINE** tuna, 2 tablespoons of the breadcrumbs, 1/2 cup of the mayonnaise, cornichons, dill, lemon juice, salt, and pepper. **WHISK** together remaining mayonnaise and the mustard, then **REFRIGERATE** until ready to use.

3. **SHAPE** tuna mixture into 6 patties, 3/4 inches thick. Place remaining breadcrumbs in a shallow dish and lightly **COAT** both sides of the patties. **REFRIGERATE** until ready to grill.

4. **BRUSH** or spray the grill grid with vegetable oil. **PREHEAT** grill to medium-high.

5. **GRILL** burgers with the grill lid down for 4 minutes per side or to desired doneness.

6. **TOP** the tuna burgers with the mustard-mayonnaise sauce and tomatoes. **SPRINKLE** with dill and **SERVE** immediately.

Backyard barbecuers can whip up an eye-catching,
crowd-pleasing meal with this well-seasoned tuna
burger, grilled corn on the cob (see page 84), and
grilled asparagus (see page 88).

A vegetarian delight, the portobello mushroom is the steak of the vegetable family

PORTOBELLO MUSHROOM BURGERS

Serves 6 ❧ Prep Time: 15 minutes ❧ Grilling Time: 7–9 minutes; high heat

INGREDIENTS

1 cup mayonnaise

1/2 cup chopped fresh basil or parsley

3 tablespoons Dijon-style mustard

1 teaspoon lemon juice

1 cup olive oil

1/2 cup balsamic vinegar

3 cloves garlic, minced

1/2 teaspoon salt

1 teaspoon pepper

6 4- to 5-inch-wide portobello mushrooms, stems removed so they are flush with the caps (see page 83)

6 large lettuce leaves

6 large slices of beefsteak tomato

6 burger buns, split and lightly grilled

1. COMBINE the mayonnaise, basil, mustard, and lemon juice in a small bowl. **MIX** well.

2. In another bowl, **COMBINE** olive oil, vinegar, garlic, salt, and pepper. **BRUSH** both sides of mushroom caps with the oil mixture.

3. PREHEAT grill to high.

4. PLACE the mushroom caps on the grill, gill-side down.

5. GRILL with the grill lid up for 4 minutes, basting with marinade, until browned.

6. TURN caps over and spoon some of the marinade over gills. **GRILL** for 3 to 4 minutes until caps are browned and very tender. (If the caps brown too much, move them to a cooler part of the grill.)

7. PLACE the lettuce, tomato, and grilled mushrooms on the toasted buns. **TOP** with mustard sauce, then **SERVE.**

Surprisingly hearty, portobellos are the most meatlike of the
mushrooms. They aren't a true variety, but simply common
button mushrooms grown to full maturity. Growers gave
portobellos their Italian name in the 1980s.

VEGETABLES

To simplify grilling, you'll need a vegetable grid
or perforated grill pan (see below)

GRILLED VEGETABLE MEDLEY

Serves 6 ➻ Prep Time: 30 minutes ➻ Marinating Time: 1–2 hours
Grilling Time: 8–10 minutes; medium-high heat

INGREDIENTS

2 red bell peppers,
cored, seeded, and cut in
quarters

1 medium zucchini,
trimmed, cut into eighths

1 medium yellow squash,
trimmed, cut into eighths

2 large Spanish or red
onions, peeled and cut
into quarters

12 shiitake mushrooms,
stems removed

1 cup olive oil

1/3 cup balsamic vinegar

1/4 cup dry sherry

3 cloves garlic, minced

3 teaspoons mixed dried
herbs such as rosemary,
basil, and oregano; or
3 tablespoons chopped
mixed fresh herbs

2 teaspoons salt

1 teaspoon pepper

I. PLACE all cut-up vegetables in a large resealable plastic bag.

2. COMBINE the olive oil, balsamic vinegar, sherry, garlic, herbs, salt, and pepper in a small bowl. **POUR** into plastic bag with vegetables. **SEAL** the bag and **TURN** to coat. Allow to **MARINATE** in the refrigerator for at least 1 hour.

3. PREHEAT grill to medium-high.

4. PLACE vegetables in a perforated grill pan and **GRILL** for 8 to 10 minutes, turning as needed, until golden brown. Or thread the vegetables onto skewers and **GRILL** for 8 minutes. **REMOVE** from heat (and if on skewers, remove from skewers with metal tongs), and **SERVE**.

What is a perforated grill pan?
If you don't have a perforated
grill pan, you should consider
purchasing one. Otherwise, you
may need to thread your vegetables
onto skewers.

Perforated grill pans, made of light-
weight aluminum, are placed directly on the grill grid.
These grill pans, with dime-size holes, are ideal for grilling
small food items like vegetables or scallops.

A colorful combo of grilled vegetables begs for
different uses. Turn it into a tempting pasta dish
by combining it with your favorite tomato sauce
and ladling it over the pasta of your choice.

Thanks to the perforated grill pan,
you can make grilled fries

GRILLED POTATOES WITH PARMESAN

Serves 6 •• Prep Time: 20 minutes •• Grilling Time: 10–12 minutes; medium heat

INGREDIENTS

3 large russet potatoes

2 tablespoons olive oil

3 to 4 cloves garlic, minced

1/2 teaspoon each salt and pepper

1/2 cup grated Parmesan cheese

1/3 cup ketchup

2 tablespoons Worcestershire sauce

1 tablespoon lemon juice

1. BRUSH or spray perforated grill pan (see page 76) with vegetable oil.

2. PREHEAT grill to medium.

3. SCRUB potatoes under cold running water and pat dry with paper towels. Do not peel.

4. CUT the potatoes lengthwise into 1/2-inch-thick slices, then cut each slice in half lengthwise again.

5. PLACE the potatoes in a large bowl and **TOSS** with the olive oil, garlic, salt, and pepper. **SPRINKLE** with the Parmesan cheese and toss gently to coat.

6. PLACE potatoes in perforated grill pan and lower grill lid.

7. GRILL the potatoes for 5 to 6 minutes on each side or until golden brown. For crispier potatoes, open the grill lid and cook for an additional 1 to 2 minutes.

8. In a small bowl, **STIR** together the ketchup, Worcestershire sauce, and lemon juice. **SERVE** with warm potatoes.

Russet Potatoes

Commercial growers in the United States classify potatoes as russet, long white, round white, and round red. The russet potato (also called the Idaho), is identifiable by its long, slightly rounded shape; brown, roughish skin; and many eyes. Russets are superior for baking and frying because they have less moisture and a higher starch content than other varieties.

Worcestershire Sauce

The exact recipe for this soy sauce-based table condiment has been kept under lock and key by manufacturer Lea and Perrins for a century and a half, but it's no secret that soy sauce, garlic, tamarind, lime juice, and anchovies contribute to its piquancy. Developed in India, the sauce takes its name from Worcester, England, where it was first bottled. In cooking, Worcestershire is used to season meats, gravies, and soups. It also sparks up the flavor of vegetable-based drinks—Bloody Marys included.

Turn summer's hands-down favorite
vegetable into a succulent side dish

GRILLED HERBED TOMATOES

Serves 6 ➤ Prep Time: 10 minutes ➤ Grilling Time: 6–8 minutes; medium-high heat

INGREDIENTS

6 large, ripe tomatoes

Salt and pepper to taste

3 tablespoons olive oil

6 cloves garlic, minced

3 teaspoons dried herbs such as thyme, basil, dill, and oregano (or a mixture); or 3 tablespoons chopped fresh herbs

3 tablespoons grated Parmesan cheese

1. SLICE tomatoes in half horizontally, parallel to the stem end, then season with salt and pepper.

2. BRUSH or spray the perforated grill pan (see page 76) with vegetable oil. **PREHEAT** grill to high.

3. In a small bowl, **COMBINE** olive oil, garlic, and herbs.

4. PLACE tomatoes on the perforated grill pan, cut-side down, and **GRILL** for 3 to 4 minutes, or until browned. Keep lid up.

5. Using tongs, **TURN** tomatoes, then spoon herb mixture over the top. Continue grilling another 3 to 4 minutes.

6. TRANSFER tomatoes to a platter and **SPRINKLE** with grated Parmesan cheese. **SERVE** immediately.

The best tomatoes for grilling are the fleshier types,
which have fewer seeds and less gel. Beefsteak
tomatoes fit the bill nicely.

To get the smokiest flavor, grill portobellos on both sides, starting with the gill side down

GRILLED MARINATED PORTOBELLO MUSHROOMS

Serves 6 ✦ Prep Time: 15 minutes ✦ Marinating Time: 1–3 hours
Grilling Time: 8–10 minutes; high heat

INGREDIENTS

6 large portobello mushrooms

3 large cloves garlic, cut into slivers

1½ cups olive oil

⅔ cup balsamic vinegar

2 teaspoons dried rosemary, crushed; or 2 tablespoons chopped fresh rosemary

2 teaspoons dried thyme or 2 tablespoons chopped fresh thyme

½ teaspoon each salt and pepper

⅔ cup grated Parmesan cheese

1. REMOVE the stems from the mushrooms (using a small, sharp knife), then discard. **WIPE** the mushrooms clean using a damp paper towel or mushroom brush. (Do not immerse mushrooms in water or they will act like sponges and become waterlogged.)

2. With the tip of a sharp paring knife, **MAKE** several slits on the gill side of the mushrooms, then insert garlic slivers.

3. COMBINE the olive oil, vinegar, herbs, salt, and pepper in a resealable plastic bag.

4. ADD mushrooms, seal bag, and carefully lay it flat in the refrigerator. **MARINATE** for up to 3 hours, turning the bag once.

5. PREHEAT grill to high.

6. REMOVE mushrooms from the bag and reserve the marinade. Arrange mushrooms on grill grid, gill-side down. Lower the lid and **GRILL** 3 to 4 minutes. Turn mushrooms over and **SPOON** some of the remaining marinade over the gills. Grill for an additional 4 minutes.

7. SPRINKLE with Parmesan cheese and **GRILL** for another 1 to 2 minutes. If the mushrooms brown too much, reduce the heat to low or move them to a cooler part of the grill. **REMOVE** from grill and **SERVE** warm.

Ask the Experts

How do I remove the odor of fresh garlic from my cutting board and hands? Lemon juice will do the trick for your hands; just squeeze some onto a paper towel and swab your fingers. To remove the odor from your cutting board, mix a little baking soda with vinegar and scrub the solution into the board with a stiff brush. Rinse well.

Portobello Mushrooms

Portobello mushrooms are simply a variety of the small white button mushroom—the cremino—grown to full maturity. The dark brown caps of the mushrooms can measure 6 inches or more in diameter and have fully exposed gills, which are key to the portobello's flavor: Exposed gills mean less moisture, which results in concentrated flavor and meaty texture. Cooked properly, a portobello cap could almost pass for a steak.

Portobellos tend to break easily, so it's a good idea to place them in a bag on a flat plate or baking dish to keep the caps from being crushed while marinating.

FIRST PERSON DISASTER

Lost-and-Found Vegetables

Everything was all set for my backyard barbecue. The burgers and dogs were on the grill, and the marinated veggies were ready to go next. I went to get my perforated grill pan, but when I walked in the kitchen I couldn't find the veggies. Where the heck had they gone?

Turns out one of my houseguests thought he would help and started grilling the vegetables directly on the grill. When I heard him yelling at it, I went over to see what was going on. A pile of vegetables was sitting on top of the hot coals—they had slipped through the grid. I laughed and handed him the grill pan. "Oh, so this is what you're supposed to use!" he chuckled.

Tom T., Washington, D.C.

Grilling corn on the cob produces a wonderful live-fire, smoky flavor

GRILLED CORN ON THE COB

Serves 6 ↠ Prep Time: 20 minutes ↠ Grilling Time: 8–12 minutes; high heat

INGREDIENTS

1 stick butter, room temperature

2 cloves garlic, minced

2 teaspoons mixed dried herbs such as dill, basil, and tarragon; or 2 tablespoons chopped fresh herbs, mixed

6 ears sweet corn, husks and silk removed

Salt and pepper to taste

I. PREHEAT grill to high.

2. In a small bowl, **COMBINE** the butter, garlic, and herbs. **BLEND** until creamy.

3. Using a pastry brush, **BRUSH** each ear of corn with some of the flavored butter.

4. GRILL corn with the grill lid down for 8 to 10 minutes or until nicely browned, turning with tongs as needed.

5. SEASON the ears with salt and pepper. **REMOVE** from grill and **SERVE** immediately.

Hot grilled corn fairly hollers, "Come and get me!" When buying
fresh corn, look for ears that are completely enclosed in green
husks, then inspect each one by pulling back a bit of the husk.
Look for kernels that are fully formed, plump, and juicy.

GRILLED SWEET POTATOES

Serves 6 ‣‣ Prep Time: 15 minutes ‣‣ Grilling Time: 35 minutes; medium-high heat

INGREDIENTS

4 medium sweet potatoes, about 4 to 5 inches long

6 tablespoons butter

3 tablespoons molasses or honey

2 tablespoons orange juice

1/2 teaspoon ground cinnamon

1/4 teaspoon each salt and pepper

1. RINSE the sweet potatoes and trim the root ends. Leave unpeeled.

2. PREHEAT grill to medium-high.

3. GRILL whole potatoes with the grill lid down for about 25 to 30 minutes or until just tender. **TURN** the potatoes several times during grilling.

4. REMOVE potatoes from grill and allow to cool slightly. **CUT** each potato into 1/2-inch-thick rounds.

5. MELT butter in a small saucepan. **REMOVE** from heat and stir in the molasses, orange juice, cinnamon, salt, and pepper.

6. BRUSH both sides of sweet potato slices with the butter mixture and **PLACE** in a perforated grill pan (see page 76). **GRILL** with lid up for 3 minutes on each side. **BASTE** with the mixture as necessary. **REMOVE** from grill and **SERVE** immediately.

Feel free to add any vegetables you like.
A combination of grilled and raw
veggies is also nice

GRILLED-VEGETABLE SALAD WITH CITRUS DRESSING

Serves 6 ⇢ Prep Time: 20 minutes ⇢ Marinating Time: 15–20 minutes
Grilling Time: 8–10 minutes; high heat

INGREDIENTS

½ cup vegetable oil

¼ cup white wine vinegar

3 tablespoons lemon or lime juice

1 teaspoon dried oregano or mint; or 1 tablespoon finely chopped fresh cilantro or mint

2 cloves garlic, minced

1 tablespoon honey

½ teaspoon each salt and pepper

3 medium zucchinis, trimmed and cut lengthwise into ¼-inch-thick slices

2 medium yellow squashes, trimmed and cut lengthwise into ¼-inch-thick slices

2 medium red onions, cut into ½-inch-thick slices

6 cups prepared salad greens

1. COMBINE the oil, vinegar, lemon juice, oregano, garlic, honey, salt, and pepper in a jar with a tight-fitting lid. Screw the lid on tightly and **SHAKE** well.

2. PLACE cut vegetables in a large bowl or large resealable plastic bag. **POUR** in ½ cup of dressing and toss. Allow vegetables to **MARINATE** for 15 to 20 minutes.

3. PREHEAT grill to high.

4. PLACE zucchinis, yellow squashes, and onions in a perforated grill pan (see page 76). **GRILL** with lid up for 4 to 5 minutes per side or until slightly charred.

5. REMOVE vegetables from grill.

6. PLACE salad greens on a large platter or in a salad bowl. **TOP** with the grilled vegetables and **TOSS** with the remaining dressing. **SERVE** immediately.

Grilling asparagus brings out its
sweetness and adds a touch of smokiness

GRILLED ASPARAGUS

Serves 6 ◆◆ Prep Time: 10 minutes ◆◆ Grilling Time: 4–6 minutes; high heat

INGREDIENTS

1½ pounds asparagus
(preferably a thicker
variety), trimmed

Toothpicks or bamboo
skewers

3 tablespoons olive oil

1½ tablespoons lemon
juice

1 shallot, minced

Salt and pepper to taste

Grated Parmesan cheese,
optional

1. PREHEAT grill to high.

2. TRIM the stem ends of each of the asparagus stalks by snapping or cutting them off.

3. LINE UP 4 asparagus stalks, tips facing the same direction. **SKEWER** them together with presoaked toothpicks or bamboo skewers (see page 23) just below and perpendicular to the tips; repeat about 2 inches from the bottom. (It should look like a minature raft.)

4. In a small bowl, **COMBINE** the olive oil, lemon juice, and shallot.

5. Using a pastry brush, **BRUSH** mixture over both sides of the asparagus. Season with salt and pepper.

6. GRILL asparagus "rafts" with the grill lid up for 2 to 3 minutes on each side or until crisp-tender.

7. REMOVE to a serving plate, then **SPRINKLE** with grated Parmesan cheese if desired. **SERVE** warm.

To keep asparagus from falling through the grill
grid, try the Japanese method of skewering
the stalks together crosswise with toothpicks
(soak the toothpicks in water first).
Another solution is to use a perforated
grill pan (see page 76).

*Sliced grilled eggplant soaks
up the smoky flavors of the grill*

GRILLED EGGPLANT WITH HERBS

Serves 6 ↦ Prep Time: 30 minutes ↦ Grilling Time: 10–15 minutes; medium-high heat

INGREDIENTS

2 1-pound eggplants, cut in ½-inch-thick rounds

2 to 4 teaspoons salt

5 tablespoons olive oil

2 teaspoons dried oregano

2 teaspoons dried thyme

1 teaspoon pepper

4 cloves garlic, minced

1. SPRINKLE eggplant slices generously with salt. Place slices on paper towels and let stand for about 20 to 30 minutes.

2. PREHEAT grill to medium-high.

3. RINSE eggplant rounds under water and pat dry with paper towels. **ARRANGE** slices on a large baking sheet and brush both sides with olive oil.

4. In a small bowl, **COMBINE** the oregano, thyme, pepper, and garlic. **SPRINKLE** both sides of the eggplant slices with the herb-garlic mixture. **ARRANGE** eggplant slices on grill grid and grill with the lid down for 5 to 8 minutes per side or until nicely browned.

5. TRANSFER eggplant rounds to a platter and **SERVE** at room temperature.

Ask the Experts

How do I choose the best eggplants?

Eggplants come in different shapes, sizes, and shades (deep purple to white), but the large, pear-shaped, dark purple variety is most typical in the United States. August to September is peak season for eggplants, and it pays to know what to look for. Choose specimens that are firm, smooth, glossy, and that feel heavy for their size; big eggplants that weigh very little may be spongy and past their prime.

Because they are very perishable and become bitter with age, eggplants should be kept in a cool, dry place and used within a day of two of purchase. If storing longer, place them in a plastic bag in the crisper drawer of the fridge.

POULTRY

LEMON GARLIC CHICKEN BREASTS

Serves 6 ↦ Prep Time: 15 minutes ↦ Marinating Time: at least 6 hours or overnight
Grilling Time: 10 minutes; medium-high heat

INGREDIENTS

¾ cup lemon juice

¾ cup olive oil

8 cloves garlic, finely chopped

3 tablespoons mixed dried herbs such as thyme, basil, oregano, parsley, and rosemary; or ⅓ cup chopped mixed fresh herbs

1½ teaspoons salt

1 teaspoon pepper

6 skinless, boneless chicken breast halves

1. COMBINE lemon juice, oil, garlic, herbs, salt, and pepper in a jar with a tight-fitting lid. Screw lid on tightly and **SHAKE** well.

2. RINSE chicken and pat dry with paper towels.

3. PLACE the chicken in a large resealable plastic bag and **POUR** in marinade. Seal the bag and turn to coat. **MARINATE** in the refrigerator for at least 6 hours or overnight.

4. BRUSH or spray the grill grid with vegetable oil. **PREHEAT** the grill to medium-high.

5. REMOVE chicken from the bag, discarding marinade.

6. GRILL chicken breasts with the grill lid up for 4 to 5 minutes on each side or until juices run clear when chicken is pierced with the tip of a sharp knife.

7. REMOVE the chicken from the grill. **CUT** diagonally into ½-inch slices or **SERVE** whole.

TIPS AND TECHNIQUES

Handling Chicken Safely

When it comes to working with chicken, you can't be too careful. Bacteria flourish in poultry at temperatures between 40° and 140° F, so don't let chicken sit out on your counter for longer than 30 minutes. It is vital that you always wash your hands and all utensils, cutting boards, plates, sponges, and anything else that comes in contact with uncooked poultry, using plenty of hot, soapy water.

The shelf life of poultry is very short, so be sure to keep it refrigerated and cook it before the "Use by" date on the package. Or freeze it until ready to use. Thaw frozen poultry in the refrigerator—allow for 5 hours per pound. A faster method calls for submerging the frozen poultry, in its package, in a large container of cold water. Change the water every half hour. Allow for 30 minutes per pound. You can also defrost it in a microwave oven. Refer to your user's manual for correct thawing times.

Ask the Experts

Does it matter that my dried herbs are several months old?

The shelf life of dried herbs is about 6 months, although you can stretch it a little longer. Just add a bit more than the recipe calls for to compensate for the weaker flavor of herbs that are past their prime.

95

This tangy marinade turns ordinary chicken into a savory feast

MAPLE MUSTARD CHICKEN

Serves 6 ⁘ Prep Time: 15 minutes ⁘ Marinating Time: at least 1 hour or overnight
Grilling Time: 8–12 minutes; medium-high heat

INGREDIENTS

¼ cup olive oil

3 large cloves garlic, coarsely chopped

2 green onions (white and green parts), finely chopped

1 teaspoon dried rosemary leaves, crumbled; or 2 tablespoons fresh rosemary, chopped

2 tablespoons cider vinegar

⅓ cup maple syrup

¼ cup Dijon-style or spicy brown mustard

½ teaspoon pepper

6 skinless, boneless chicken breast halves

1. HEAT oil in a medium skillet over medium-high heat. **ADD** garlic and green onions and **SAUTÉ** for 2 minutes, stirring constantly. **ADD** herbs and vinegar and **COOK** for 30 seconds. Remove from heat and **WHISK** in maple syrup and mustard, then stir in the pepper.

2. RINSE chicken and pat dry with paper towels.

3. PLACE chicken in a large resealable plastic bag and **POUR** in marinade. Seal the bag and **TURN** to coat. Place chicken in the refrigerator and **MARINATE** for at least 1 hour or overnight.

4. BRUSH or spray grill grid with vegetable oil. **PREHEAT** grill to medium-high.

5. REMOVE chicken from bag, discarding marinade. **GRILL** chicken breasts with lid up for about 4 to 5 minutes per side or until juices run clear when the chicken is pierced with the tip of a sharp knife. **SERVE** warm.

Ask the Experts

Does it matter whether maple syrup is "real"? When it is part of a cooked sauce like the one used in this recipe, you may not be able to tell the difference between **real maple syrup** (the concentrated sap from the maple tree) or **maple-flavored syrup** (corn syrup or another less costly syrup flavored with a little maple syrup). Avoid using **pan-cake syrups** in sauces; in most cases, they are merely corn syrup flavored with artificial maple extract.

Cider Vinegar

This fruity vinegar, made from fermented apple cider, was once primarily produced by apple growers in the northeastern United States and the French province of Normandy. Apple cider vinegar is popular for not only its flavor but also its supposed health-giving properties. It is also less expensive than most vinegars.

This is a refreshing dish—a little sweet, a little tangy

GRILLED CITRUS CHICKEN

Serves 6 ▸▸ Prep Time: 15 minutes ▸▸ Marinating Time: at least 1 hour
Grilling Time: 10 minutes; high heat

INGREDIENTS

1 cup orange juice

⅓ cup lime juice

1 20-ounce can crushed pineapple, in juice

2 cloves garlic, minced

2 tablespoons soy sauce

2 tablespoons honey

2 tablespoons olive or vegetable oil

1 teaspoon dried basil or 2 tablespoons chopped fresh basil

6 large, skinless, boneless, chicken breast halves

1. In a resealable plastic bag, **COMBINE** the orange juice, lime juice, crushed pineapple, garlic, soy, honey, oil, and basil. **RESERVE** ¼ cup of the marinade for basting.

2. RINSE the chicken and pat dry with paper towels. **PLACE** chicken in a resealable bag and **ADD** all but reserved marinade. Seal the bag and turn to coat. **MARINATE** in refrigerator for at least 1 hour or up to 6 hours.

3. BRUSH or spray the grill grid with vegetable oil. **PREHEAT** grill to high.

4. REMOVE chicken from the bag, discarding the marinade.

5. GRILL chicken with lid up for 5 minutes per side, basting with the reserved marinade. Juices should run clear when meat is pierced with the tip of a sharp knife. **SERVE** warm.

Kitchen Knives

Several different knives are used in cooking, and for good reason: The right knife makes food preparation easier and does the job better, whether you're chopping onions or slicing bread.

How many kitchen knives does a cook need—and which kind? The average cook can get by with two: a cook's knife and a paring knife. **Cook's knives** (sometimes called chef's knives) are used for chopping and slicing and usually have 8- to 10-inch-long blades. Besides being long enough to chop food in a rapid up-and-down motion, the tapered blade allows you to chop using a rocking motion. (With either motion, you press down firmly on the top of the blade with your palm.)

Cook's Knife

Serrated Knife

Paring knives (also called utility knives) are smaller versions of cook's knives, with 3- or 4-inch-long blades. Unlike a cook's knife, which is an "impact tool," parers are used for peeling or scraping fruits and vegetables and for trimming the fat from meat, among other things.

A third choice, **serrated knives**, are best for slicing bread and soft fruits and vegetables. When the knife is used with a push-and-pull stroke, its sawlike edge slices without mashing or compacting the food.

As important as having the right knife is keeping it sharp. Sharpening tools range from the long-used **whetstone** to **electric sharpeners** to the **steel**, a handheld tool with a ridged steel shaft.

Paring Knife

DOWN-HOME BARBECUED CHICKEN

Serves 6–8 ▸▸ Prep Time: 15–20 minutes ▸▸ Marinating Time: 1–4 hours
Grilling Time: 20–24 minutes; medium heat

INGREDIENTS

1½ cups ketchup

½ cup pineapple juice or orange juice

4½ tablespoons Worcestershire sauce

2 tablespoons brown sugar

2 tablespoons cider vinegar

2 tablespoons rum or Scotch

1 teaspoon ground ginger

1 teaspoon garlic powder

Salt and pepper to taste

8 to 10 pieces of chicken legs, breasts, or thighs, bone in and skin on

FOR THE BARBECUE SAUCE

1. COMBINE the ketchup, pineapple juice, Worcestershire sauce, sugar, vinegar, rum, ginger, and garlic powder in a medium saucepan. Bring to a **BOIL** over medium heat, stirring.

2. Lower the heat to low and **SIMMER** for about 10 to 15 minutes, until slightly thickened. Season with salt and pepper, and cool slightly.

3. TRANSFER to a bowl, cover, and **REFRIGERATE** until ready to use. (Sauce can be kept in the refrigerator for up to 2 weeks.)

FOR THE CHICKEN

1. RINSE the chicken and pat dry with paper towels.

2. PLACE chicken pieces in a resealable plastic bag and **POUR** in ¾ of the barbecue sauce. **SEAL** bag and **TURN** to coat. Let marinate for 1 to 4 hours. **RESERVE** remaining sauce.

3. BRUSH or spray the grill grid with vegetable oil. **PREHEAT** grill to medium.

4. REMOVE the chicken from the bag and place chicken pieces, skin-side up, on grill grid and **GRILL** with the lid down for 10 to 12 minutes, using tongs to turn chicken every few minutes. **BRUSH** chicken with reserved sauce, and continue grilling another 10 minutes or until the skin is browned and the juices run clear when meat is pierced with the tip of a sharp knife.

5. REMOVE chicken pieces from grill and **SERVE.**

An American classic, barbecued chicken tastes even better when served with another down-home favorite: corn on the cob (see page 84). Cole slaw is another traditional side dish. Just be sure the slaw's dressing isn't so tangy that it competes with the barbecue sauce. A milder dressing, or even one on the sweet side, is a better choice.

GRILLED MUSTARD CHICKEN

Serves 6 ◆◆ Prep Time: 10 minutes ◆◆ Cooking Time: 25 minutes
Grilling Time: 10 minutes; high heat

INGREDIENTS

2 14.5-ounce cans reduced-sodium chicken broth

3 tablespoons dry vermouth or white wine

2 tablespoons Dijon-style mustard

2 tablespoons honey mustard

1/4 teaspoon pepper

6 large skinless, boneless chicken breast halves

1 tablespoon olive oil

3 cloves garlic, minced

Salt and pepper, to taste

FOR THE SAUCE

1. COMBINE broth and vermouth in a medium saucepan over high heat. Bring to a **BOIL** for 1 minute, then **LOWER** heat and cook 20 to 25 minutes or until the liquid is reduced to 1½ cups.

2. REDUCE heat to low and **WHISK** in the 2 mustards. **SIMMER** for 2 to 3 minutes until slightly thickened, then **STIR** in pepper.

3. REMOVE from heat. If preparing ahead, transfer sauce to a bowl or jar, cover, and refrigerate until ready to use (sauce will keep for 3 days). Reheat before serving.

FOR THE CHICKEN

1. RINSE the chicken and pat dry with paper towels.

2. BRUSH or spray the grill grid with vegetable oil. **PREHEAT** the grill to high.

3. RUB both sides of the chicken breasts with oil and garlic. Season with salt and pepper.

4. GRILL with the lid up for 5 minutes per side or until the juices run clear when the breasts are pierced with the tip of a sharp knife.

5. REHEAT sauce by microwaving uncovered on high for 1 to 2 minutes, then **SPOON** over chicken breasts and **SERVE** warm.

Grilling Over Wood

Wood chunks will ratchet up the flavor of grilled foods another notch, providing that magic finishing touch. They are sold in bags and can either be placed on top of charcoal (in which case they should be soaked in water for 30 minutes beforehand) or used as the sole fuel.

Strong-flavored **hardwoods**—in descending order, mesquite, hickory, red oak, pecan, walnut, and chestnut—are best for red meats and game. Milder woods complement the flavors of poultry and fish and come in two types: **fruit woods** (including cherry, apple, pear, peach, and mulberry) and **nonfruiting hardwoods** (maple, alder, sweet birch, beech, baywood, sassafras, and ash).

If you have any of these trees on your property and want to make use of fallen branches, be aware that wood used for grilling has a shelf life. Before being chunked or chipped, branches 3 or 4 inches in diameter should age for at least 3 months and then be used within 6 to 8 months; otherwise, they're flavorless. Twigs will dry much faster; use any that are no longer "green."

A caution: Don't use wood chunks from softwoods like pine or fir. Their resin makes the smoke sooty and potentially harmful.

Mesquite Chunks

A delicious syrup of balsamic vinegar and sugar adds a complex flavor to ordinary chicken

CHICKEN BREASTS IN BALSAMIC SYRUP

Serves 6 ◆▸ Prep Time: 20 minutes ◆▸ Grilling Time: 10 minutes; high heat

INGREDIENTS

2 cups balsamic vinegar

$2/3$ cup honey

$1/3$ cup white granulated sugar

$1/3$ cup brown sugar

$1/2$ cup soy sauce

6 skinless, boneless, chicken breast halves

1 to **2** tablespoons olive oil

Salt and pepper, to taste

FOR THE SYRUP

1. In a medium heavy saucepan, **COMBINE** balsamic vinegar, honey, sugars, and soy sauce. Bring to a boil over medium heat.

2. REDUCE heat to low and **SIMMER** sauce for about 15 minutes or until reduced to $1\frac{1}{2}$ cups. **SKIM** off any foam that appears on surface. **POUR** mixture through a strainer into a jar and **COOL** to room temperature. Seal jar.

FOR THE CHICKEN

1. BRUSH or spray the grill grid with vegetable oil. **PREHEAT** the grill to high.

2. RINSE chicken and pat dry with paper towels.

3. RUB both sides of the chicken breasts with olive oil, then season with salt and pepper.

4. GRILL chicken with lid up for 5 minutes on each side or until juices run clear when the meat is pierced with the tip of a sharp knife.

5. DRIZZLE chicken with balsamic syrup. **SERVE** warm.

TIPS AND TECHNIQUES

Ask the Experts

My box of brown sugar hardened after a few weeks in the cupboard. How do I resoften it?

To turn hardened brown sugar soft again, break the block into large chunks and put them in a plastic bag along with a good-size wedge of apple. Seal the bag airtight. The sugar should resoften in 1 or 2 days. To resoften faster, microwave for 1 minute.

What's the difference between light and dark brown sugar?

In its modern form, brown sugar is usually white sugar coated with molasses—therefore, the lighter the sugar, the more delicate the flavor. Brown sugars come in several shades, with the very dark "old-fashioned" sugar tasting primarily of molasses.

Balsamic Vinegar

An Italian specialty, balsamic vinegar is made from white Trebbiano grape juice. Its dark color is explained by the vinegar's years-long aging in barrels. Aging also accounts for its distinctive pungency and sweetness.

Teriyaki sauce—a blend of honey, soy sauce, and sesame oil—goes equally well with meat, poultry, seafood, and vegetables

CHICKEN TERIYAKI

Serves 4 ◆◆ Prep Time: 20 minutes, ◆◆ Marinating Time: at least 6 hours
Grilling Time: 20–25 minutes; medium heat

INGREDIENTS

½ cup soy sauce

½ cup dry sherry

¼ cup plus 1 tablespoon honey

¼ cup sesame or canola oil

½ cup orange juice

4 cloves garlic, minced

1 teaspoon ground ginger; or 1 tablespoon minced fresh ginger

1 3½- to 4-pound chicken, split in half

1. In a medium bowl, **WHISK** together soy sauce, sherry, honey, sesame oil, orange juice, garlic, and ginger. Reserve ¼ cup of the marinade for basting.

2. RINSE chicken and pat dry with paper towels.

3. PLACE the chicken halves in two separate large resealable plastic bags and **DIVIDE** the marinade evenly between each. Seal the bags and **TURN** to coat. **MARINATE** in the refrigerator for at least 6 hours or overnight.

4. BRUSH or spray the grill grid with vegetable oil. **PREHEAT** grill to medium.

5. REMOVE chicken from the bags, discarding the marinade. **PLACE** chicken on grill, skin-side down.

6. GRILL chicken with lid down for 10 to 12 minutes on each side, basting frequently with the reserved marinade. Juices should run clear when the meat is pierced with the tip of a sharp knife. **SERVE** warm.

Macaroni salad and sliced garden-fresh tomatoes add an American touch to Chicken Teriyaki. A gift from the Japanese, teriyaki is a marinade that was traditionally made with soy sauce, ginger, and sugar, often with a few other seasonings thrown in. It's the sugar in the marinade that gives chicken and other cooked foods a slight glaze.

ORANGE AND BRANDY GRILLED CHICKEN

Serves 6 ◆◆ Prep Time: 20 minutes ◆◆ Marinating Time: at least 3 hours
Grilling Time: 10 minutes; high heat

INGREDIENTS

3/4 cup orange juice

2/3 cup balsamic vinegar

1/3 cup molasses or maple syrup

1/4 cup brandy

6 cloves garlic, minced

1 teaspoon hot red pepper sauce

6 skinless, boneless chicken breast halves

Vegetable oil

Salt and pepper to taste

FOR THE MARINADE AND SAUCE

1. In a medium saucepan, **COMBINE** the orange juice, balsamic vinegar, molasses, brandy, garlic, and hot red pepper sauce and bring to a **BOIL** over medium-high heat.

2. Reduce heat to medium-low and **SIMMER** for 10 minutes or until slightly reduced. Remove marinade from heat and **COOL** to room temperature.

3. SET ASIDE 1/2 cup of the marinade to use as sauce.

FOR THE CHICKEN

1. RINSE chicken and pat dry with paper towels.

2. PLACE chicken breasts in a large resealable plastic bag. **POUR** marinade over the chicken, then seal bag and **TURN** to coat. **REFRIGERATE** for at least 3 to 24 hours.

3. BRUSH or spray the grill grid with vegetable oil. **PREHEAT** the grill to high.

4. REMOVE chicken from the bag, discarding marinade.

5. SEASON the chicken with salt and pepper, and **GRILL** 5 minutes per side or until juices run clear when meat is pierced with the tip of a sharp knife.

6. MICROWAVE reserved marinade on high for 1 minute. **CUT** chicken crosswise on a diagonal into 1/2-inch slices and **SPOON** a small amount of sauce over each breast. **SERVE** warm.

About Brandy

Teetotalers should know that the alcohol in brandy evaporates during the cooking process—something that's true of every alcoholic beverage. Thankfully, the smoky, slightly sweet flavor stays around to work its magic. Aged in wood, brandies are distilled from wine or other fermented fruit juices. The Calvados brandy of Normandy, for example, is apple-based.

The word "brandy" (from the Dutch *brandewijin*, meaning "burned wine") generally refers only to brandy made from grapes. When made from other fruits, the fruit's name is added: apple brandy, pear brandy, and so forth. Two fine brandies are named for their places of origin: Cognac and Armagnac, both towns in France.

Grading Molasses

Most supermarkets carry molasses, a sweetener made from the juice pressed from sugar cane. The juice is slowly cooked until much of the moisture evaporates, making the syrup dark and very thick.

Light molasses (from the first boiling of the sugar syrup) or **dark molasses** (from the second) can be used in this recipe, although the dark kind imparts a more robust flavor. Some health food aficionados prefer a third type: **blackstrap** molasses. From the third boiling (and in a way the dregs of the barrel), this syrup is so dark, thick, and often bitter that it is more frequently used as an additive to cattle fodder.

CHICKEN WITH PINEAPPLE GLAZE

Serves 6 ➻ Prep Time: 30 minutes ➻ Grilling Time: 20 minutes; medium heat

INGREDIENTS

3 tablespoons vegetable oil

2 medium-size sweet onions, thinly sliced

2 cloves garlic, minced

6 boneless chicken breast halves, skin on

Salt and pepper to taste

6 pineapple slices, canned or fresh

Toothpicks

Pineapple Glaze
(see opposite page for recipe)

1. HEAT the oil in a large skillet over medium heat. **SAUTÉ** onions and garlic for 3 minutes, stirring occasionally. **REMOVE** from heat and set aside.

2. RINSE chicken and pat dry with paper towels.

3. PLACE chicken breast halves skin-side down on work surface. Place a sheet of plastic wrap over the chicken breasts and **POUND** lightly with the back of a heavy frying pan or meat mallet until they are 1/4-inch thick. Season with salt and pepper.

4. SPREAD an equal amount of onion and garlic mixture over each chicken breast and **TOP** with one pineapple slice. (If using canned slices, reserve juice for glaze.) **FOLD** half of the chicken breast over the filling, then secure it with toothpicks. Set aside.

5. BRUSH or spray the grill grid with vegetable oil. **PREHEAT** grill to medium.

6. BRUSH both sides of chicken with the Pineapple Glaze and **GRILL** with the lid down for 10 minutes. **TURN** over, brush with more glaze, and **GRILL** 8 to 10 minutes longer or until juices run clear when the meat is pierced with the tip of a knife. **SERVE**.

Pineapple Glaze

1 cup pineapple juice; or reserved juice from 16-ounce can of pineapple slices

1½ tablespoons honey

½ cup reduced-sodium chicken broth

1 teaspoon garlic powder

1 teaspoon cornstarch mixed with 1 tablespoon cold water (to make cornstarch paste)

1. COMBINE the pineapple juice, honey, broth, and garlic powder in a small saucepan and **COOK** over low heat until simmering.

2. WHISK in cornstarch paste. **COOK** about 2 minutes, stirring, until slightly thickened. **REMOVE** from heat and set aside until using in Step 6 of the recipe on the opposite page.

Sweet Treats

Sweet onions are one of the treats of spring, right up there with asparagus. Two towns that lay claim to the sweetest onions, grown in low-sulfite soil, are Vidalia, Georgia, and Walla Walla, Washington. The easier-to-find Vidalia onions are large, pale yellow, and very juicy; they're available in supermarkets from May through June. Walla Walla onions are large, rounder, and golden. Their season is June through September, but outside of the Pacific Northwest, they usually have to be bought by mail order. These and other sweet onion varieties get their sweetness not just from their higher sugar content but also from lower levels of sulfur.

Fresh tarragon is essential for this delicious chicken dish

FRESH TARRAGON AND MUSTARD CHICKEN

Serves 6 •• Prep Time: 10 minutes •• Marinating Time: 2–4 hours
Grilling Time: 25–30 minutes; medium-high heat

INGREDIENTS

¹/₂ cup chopped fresh tarragon

¹/₃ cup Dijon-style mustard

¹/₃ cup dry sherry

1¹/₂ tablespoons olive oil

2 tablespoons honey

1 small shallot, peeled

¹/₂ teaspoon each salt and pepper

6 pounds chicken pieces such as legs, thighs, wings, and breasts

Salt and pepper to taste

1. COMBINE tarragon, mustard, sherry, oil, honey, shallot, salt, and pepper in a blender or in the bowl of a food processor with a steel blade. **BLEND** or process until smooth. **RESERVE** ¹/₂ cup for basting.

2. RINSE chicken and pat dry with paper towels.

3. DIVIDE chicken pieces into two groups and place each group in a large resealable plastic bag. **DIVIDE** marinade evenly and **POUR** over chicken pieces. Seal bags and **TURN** to coat.

4. MARINATE chicken for 2 to 4 hours in refrigerator, turning the bags once or twice.

5. BRUSH or spray the grill grid with vegetable oil. **PREHEAT** the grill to medium-high.

6. REMOVE chicken from the bag, discarding the marinade.

7. GRILL chicken with the lid down for about 25 minutes, turning and **BASTING** with reserved marinade every 5 minutes. Chicken is done when juices run clear when meat is pierced with the tip of a sharp knife.

8. REMOVE from grill and **SERVE**.

Tarragon Tips

As herbs go, tarragon is as French as they come, taking pride of place in Béarnaise sauce and the classic herb mix *fines herbes*. But use it sparingly: Tarragon's taste, reminiscent of licorice, is aromatic enough to dominate other flavors in a dish. Fresh tarragon is preferred over dried because drying compromises the flavor.

FIRST PERSON DISASTER

Got Sauce?

I was running late. The first thing I did when I got home was make a salad dressing and a marinade. I knew that my friends would walk through the door at any minute, ready for dinner. I made a marinade and poured it over the chicken, then finished making the salad while entertaining my guests. Since we all had to work the next day, I knew everyone would want to eat ASAP, so I cranked up the gas grill and put the chicken on, even though it had marinated for only a few minutes. I figured, how bad could it be?

When the chicken had finished grilling, I took it off the grill and sliced one of the breasts. I tried a bite. It wasn't great—the chicken hadn't marinated long enough to absorb anything, and I'd cooked it too long to boot! I have very gracious friends who willingly ate the dried-out chicken, which I think they soaked in their salad dressing! Next time, I'll allow more time for marinating and a little less grill time!

Keith S., Bellmore, New York

Canned or frozen peaches will do the trick in this dish, but you can use fresh if you'd prefer

GRILLED CHICKEN WITH PEACH GLAZE

Serves 6 ◆◆ Prep Time: 20 minutes ◆◆ Grilling Time: 20 minutes; medium heat

INGREDIENTS

3 tablespoons canola oil

2 medium-size red onions, chopped

4 cloves garlic, minced

6 boneless, skinless chicken breast halves

Salt and pepper to taste

1 16-ounce can sliced peaches, juice reserved

Toothpicks

2 tablespoons honey

1/2 cup canned low-sodium chicken broth

1/4 cup dry sherry or white wine

1 teaspoon garlic powder

1/2 teaspoon each salt and pepper

1 teaspoon cornstarch mixed with 1 tablespoon cold water (to make cornstarch paste)

1. HEAT oil in a large skillet over medium heat. **ADD** onions and garlic and **SAUTÉ** over low heat for 3 minutes, stirring often. **REMOVE** onions and garlic from heat and set aside.

2. PLACE chicken breast halves on work surface and **FLATTEN** them with your fingers. Season with salt and pepper. **SPREAD** an equal amount of onion-garlic mixture over each chicken breast and **TOP** each with 2 or 3 peach slices.

3. FOLD each chicken breast over, overlapping the ends. **SECURE** with toothpicks and set the chicken breasts aside.

4. In a small saucepan, **WHISK** together 1/2 cup of the peach juice and the honey, chicken broth, sherry, garlic powder, salt, and pepper. **COOK** over low heat until combined. **WHISK** in cornstarch paste, stirring until slightly thickened.

5. BRUSH or spray the grill grid with vegetable oil. **PREHEAT** the grill to medium.

6. BRUSH both sides of chicken with some of the glaze, then **GRILL** with the lid down for 8 to 10 minutes. **TURN** over, brush with more glaze, and grill for another 10 minutes or until juices run clear when meat is pierced with the tip of a sharp knife. **REMOVE** from grill and **SERVE** warm with the remaining sauce.

An all-grilled plate of peach-glazed chicken, vegetables, and new potatoes skewered on a sprig of
rosemary is a credit to any backyard barbecuer. This cook used peeled fresh peaches
for the garnish. To peel a peach, first bring a pot of water to a boil. Then use a sharp knife to
make an X in the base of the peach. Using a slotted spoon, lower the peach into the boiling water
for no more than 60 seconds. Immediately transfer the peach to a bowl of ice water.
When the peach cools, you'll be able to peel it easily with your fingers.

The chickens are split in half to make them
thin enough to grill over direct heat

GRILLED PESTO CHICKEN

Serves 6 •• Prep Time: 15 minutes •• Marinating Time: at least 2 hours
Grilling Time: 25–30 minutes; medium-high heat

INGREDIENTS

2 3- to 4-pound chickens, each split in half

2 cups prepared or homemade pesto (see recipe on
opposite page)

1. RINSE chickens and pat dry with paper towels.

2. Using a rubber spatula or a large spoon, **SPREAD** 1¹/₂ cups of
the pesto over the chickens, evenly coating both sides. **RESERVE**
remaining pesto.

3. PLACE chickens in 2 large glass baking dishes. **COVER** with
plastic wrap, then **MARINATE** in the refrigerator for at least
2 hours or overnight. **TURN** chickens over occasionally to ensure
even marination.

4. BRUSH or spray the grill grid with vegetable oil. **PREHEAT**
grill to medium-high.

5. PLACE chickens on grill grid skin-side down and **GRILL** with
lid down for 12 to 15 minutes. Turn chicken over and **SPREAD**
reserved pesto on top. To minimize flare-ups (sudden bursts of
flame caused by bits of food or grease that have dropped onto
the coals), move the chicken to a cooler location on the grill if
necessary.

6. GRILL another 12 to 15 minutes or until juices run clear when
meat is pierced with the tip of a sharp knife.

7. TRANSFER chicken to a platter, **CUT** into pieces, and **SERVE**
warm.

About Pesto

The traditional recipe for pesto sauce originated in Genoa, Italy. It was an uncooked mix of fresh basil, garlic, pine nuts, cheese (Parmesan or pecorino), and olive oil. Today, the name "pesto" is given to any number of uncooked sauces that have much the same ingredients but replace basil with another herb, such as cilantro or mint. The recipe on this page is a variation of the original.

Fresh Pesto

2 cups fresh basil leaves, rinsed and dried

3 cloves garlic

¼ cup pine nuts

½ cup grated Parmesan or Romano cheese

2 tablespoons olive oil

1. COMBINE basil, garlic, pine nuts, and cheese in the bowl of a food processor fitted with a steel blade, then **PROCESS** until the ingredients are coarsely chopped.

2. With the machine running, **ADD** oil a teaspoon at a time and **PROCESS** until smooth. If mixture is too thick, add a little water.

GRILLED CORNISH GAME HENS

Serves 6 ◆◆ Prep Time: 10 minutes ◆◆ Grilling Time: 40 minutes; medium-high heat

INGREDIENTS

3 1¼- to 1½-pound Cornish game hens, cut in half

Salt and pepper to taste

6 tablespoons butter

2 tablespoons vegetable oil

1½ teaspoons curry powder

1½ teaspoons ground coriander

1½ teaspoons ground cumin

1 teaspoon chili powder

6 cloves garlic, very finely chopped

1. BRUSH or spray the grill grid with vegetable oil. **PREHEAT** the grill to medium-high.

2. REMOVE the innards from inside hens and discard. **RINSE** hens well, inside and out, and pat dry with paper towels. **SEASON** with salt and pepper.

3. COMBINE the butter with the oil in a small saucepan. **MELT** over moderate heat and **STIR** in spices and garlic. Remove from heat and **BRUSH** some of the spice mixture over the hens.

4. Place hens on grill, skin-side down, and **GRILL** with lid down for 10 minutes. **TURN** hens over with tongs, then **BASTE** with spice mixture. **GRILL** for 20 minutes, basting with spice mixture. Continue grilling another 10 minutes longer, without basting, or until juices run clear when meat is pierced with the tip of a sharp knife.

5. REMOVE hens from grill and **SERVE** warm.

TIPS AND TECHNIQUES

Curry Powder

Though commercial curry powder doesn't have the fabulous flavor of the blends pulverized daily in India, it can still do wonders for a dish.

There are as many blends of the 20 main spices that go into curry as there are cooks. Some of the most commonly used ingredients are fenugreek, cumin, cinnamon, fennel seed, mace, cardamom, coriander, tamarind, turmeric, and saffron—the last two being responsible for the characteristic yellow color of curry dishes.

Curry powder bought at supermarkets is generally of two types—**standard** and the hotter **Madras**. Both lose their pungency in about two months, so store them airtight—and think about browsing through Indian cookbooks in hopes of finding a way to keep this fragrant herb from going to waste!

Ask the Experts

What's a Cornish hen?
This small game hen is a cross between two chickens, the Cornish and the white rock—the reason its alternate name is rock Cornish game hen. Processed when 4 to 6 weeks old, the hens weigh from 1 to 2 pounds; the smaller the size, the more delicate the meat. Cornish hens are sold fresh or frozen. Thaw frozen hens overnight in the refrigerator before cooking.

Serve this chicken salad with your favorite
dressing or try the one given here

GRILLED-CHICKEN SALAD

Serves 6 ·▸ Prep Time: 15 minutes ·▸ Grilling Time: 10 minutes; high heat

INGREDIENTS

6 skinless, boneless chicken breast halves

Olive oil for rubbing

Salt and pepper to taste

1/4 cup lemon juice

1 clove garlic, minced

1/4 teaspoon each salt and pepper

3/4 cup olive oil

1 1/2 cups crumbled feta cheese

12 cups mixed lettuces, torn

1 red bell pepper, cored, seeded, and thinly sliced

1 yellow bell pepper, cored, seeded, and thinly sliced

1 small seedless cucumber, cut into thin rounds

1 small red onion, thinly sliced

FOR THE CHICKEN

1. BRUSH or spray the grill grid with vegetable oil, then **PRE-HEAT** the grill to high.

2. RINSE chicken breasts and pat dry with paper towels. **RUB** the chicken with olive oil and season with salt and pepper.

3. GRILL chicken with lid up for 5 minutes on each side or until juices run clear when meat is pierced with the tip of a sharp knife.

4. REMOVE from grill and let cool slightly. **CUT** chicken breasts crosswise on the diagonal into 1/2-inch slices and set aside.

FOR THE DRESSING AND SALAD

1. In a small bowl, **COMBINE** the lemon juice, garlic, salt, and pepper. **WHISK** in olive oil, combining thoroughly. Gently **FOLD** in the feta cheese. Set aside.

2. In a large bowl, **COMBINE** the mixed lettuces, bell peppers, cucumber, and onion.

3. DIVIDE the salad equally among 6 plates and **TOP** with the grilled chicken breast slices. **DRIZZLE** with the feta-lemon dressing and **SERVE** immediately.

Mixed Lettuces

Gone are the days when making a salad meant washing lettuce leaves and patting them dry one by one. Today you'll find ready-to-toss leaves washed, dried, and prepackaged in the produce section of your grocery store.

Another cook's habit that hasn't so much gone by the board as skirted it: using only one type of lettuce in a salad. Now Bibb pairs happily with Boston, romaine with red leaf. Moreover, lettuce has been joined in the salad bowl by endive, escarole, and other chicories; the slightly peppery arugula; and even dandelion greens.

Mesclun, the name given to a gourmet mix of salad greens picked young, commonly includes oak-leaf lettuce, mâche, radicchio, sorrel, frisée, and the aforementioned arugula and dandelion, among other trendy greens.

Seeding Peppers

To seed bell peppers, use a sharp knife to slice off the top and stem, then cut the pepper in half lengthwise. Use a spoon or melon baller to scoop out the seeds and whitish membrane. Alternately, slice the whole pepper in half lengthwise, then cut out the stalk before proceeding as above.

MEAT

PEPPER-CRUSTED NEW YORK STRIP

Serves 6 ⟶ Prep Time: 5 minutes ⟶ Refrigeration Time: 1 hour
Grilling Time: 8–10 minutes; high heat

INGREDIENTS

1 stick butter, room temperature

2 cloves garlic, minced

1 tablespoon mixed dried herbs such as parsley, basil, oregano, and chives; or 4 tablespoons finely chopped fresh mixed herbs

6 tablespoons peppercorns, coarsely ground

1 teaspoon coarse salt

6 1-inch-thick boneless New York strip steaks, about 6 to 8 ounces each

FOR THE GARLIC-HERB BUTTER

1. In a small bowl, thoroughly **COMBINE** the butter, garlic, and herbs.

2. MOUND butter mixture on a sheet of wax paper, then **ROLL** into a 1-inch-wide cylinder. **CHILL** in refrigerator for up to 1 hour. When ready to use, unwrap and **CUT** into 1/2-inch-thick rounds.

FOR THE STEAKS

1. Coarsely **GRIND** peppercorns in a pepper mill, electric coffee grinder, or food processor. **COMBINE** with coarse salt and use your fingers to press mixture evenly onto both sides of steaks.

2. BRUSH or spray the grill grid with vegetable oil. **PREHEAT** the grill to high.

3. GRILL with lid down for 4 to 5 minutes on each side for medium-rare.

4. REMOVE steaks from grill and let rest for 2 to 3 minutes. **TOP** each steak with 1 round of Garlic-Herb-Butter and **SERVE** immediately.

TIPS AND TECHNIQUES

Ask the Experts

Why top steak with butter?
While it may seem a bit decadent to add more fat to a grilled steak, herb butter is a wonderful flavor enhancer. It also makes steak taste even juicier.

How do I get the crosshatch marks that I see on steaks served in restaurants?
If you want to create those classic grilled steak marks, grill the steak at an angle to the bars of the grid (with one end at the 2 o'clock mark of an imaginary clock) for 2 to 3 minutes. Then, using tongs, rotate it so the end is at the 6 o'clock mark. Repeat the process after turning the steaks. You can also use this method when grilling pork, veal chops, chicken breasts, and fish steaks.

What is New York strip steak?
New York strip steak is one of several names for a cut that comes from the short loin, the most tender section of beef. In meat markets and on menus, the cut also goes by the name of strip steak, shell steak, sirloin club steak, Kansas City strip steak, and Delmonico steak.

Drip Pans

Aluminum foil drip pans, available in several sizes at supermarkets and barbecue stores, are a must when you're grilling fatty foods. When using a charcoal grill, set the pan on the charcoal grate directly under the food, and bank the coals around the side of the pan. With gas grills, the pan is set directly on the lava rock or ceramic briquettes under the food being grilled.

This recipe calls for rib-eye or T-bone steaks

THE PERFECT STEAK

Serves 6 ➻ Prep Time: 10 minutes ➻ Marinating Time: 15–20 minutes
Grilling Time: 12–14 minutes; high heat

INGREDIENTS

1/4 cup Worcestershire sauce

3 tablespoons dry mustard

2 cloves garlic, minced

2 tablespoons lime or lemon juice

Salt and pepper to taste

6 1 1/2-inch-thick T-bone or rib-eye steaks

1. COMBINE the Worcestershire sauce, mustard, garlic, lime juice, salt, and pepper.

2. PLACE steaks on a platter and use the back of a spoon to **SPREAD** the mixture evenly on both sides.

3. BRUSH or spray the grill grid with vegetable oil.

4. PREHEAT grill to high. As grill heats, let steaks **MARINATE** at room temperature for 15 to 20 minutes.

5. GRILL steak with lid down for 6 to 7 minutes on each side for medium rare or to desired doneness.

6. TRANSFER steaks to a platter and let rest for 2 to 3 minutes.

7. SERVE steaks whole or thinly sliced on the diagonal.

Slicing a steak before serving shows off the main attraction—
meat grilled to perfection. T-bone steaks are cut from the center of the
short loin. A rib-eye steak is exceptionally tender meat.

The sherry-enhanced marinade in this dish is also good for chicken, beef tenderloin, and lamb chops

ASIAN FLANK STEAK

Serves 6–8 ♦ Prep Time: 15 minutes ♦ Marinating Time: 4–24 hours
Grilling Time: 6 minutes; medium-high heat

INGREDIENTS

½ cup soy sauce

½ cup sesame or olive oil

⅔ cup dry sherry

½ cup orange juice

¼ cup plus 1 tablespoon honey

4 cloves garlic

6 green onions (white and green parts), finely chopped

1 tablespoon powdered ginger or 1 1-inch-thick piece of fresh ginger, peeled and coarsely chopped (see page 29)

2 1-pound flank steaks

1. To make the marinade, **COMBINE** the soy sauce, sesame oil, sherry, orange juice, honey, garlic, green onions, and ginger in a blender or food processor. **BLEND** until pureed.

2. PLACE flank steaks in 2 large plastic resealable plastic bags. **DIVIDE** the marinade evenly and pour it into the bags. Seal the bags, then **TURN** several times to coat.

3. PLACE bags in refrigerator. **MARINATE** steaks for at least 4 hours or as long as 24 hours.

4. BRUSH or spray the grill grid with vegetable oil, then **PRE-HEAT** grill to medium-high.

5. REMOVE steaks from bags, discarding the marinade. **GRILL** steaks with lid up for about 3 minutes on each side for medium rare or to desired doneness. Thinly slice steak across the grain at a 45-degree angle—if you slice it with the grain, it will be chewy. **SERVE** warm.

Ask the Experts

What is flank steak?
Flank steak is a thin, fibrous cut of beef. Although it is quite flavorful, it is not naturally tender. This explains why recipes using the steak call for a tenderizing marinade before the steak is grilled or broiled. Flank steak is best served rare to medium-rare.

Can I substitute cooking sherry for dry sherry?
It's better not to, since cooking sherry is sherry with added salt. Besides, cooking sherry is not very tasty. True sherry, which originated in the Andalusia region of Spain, is a wine that has been fortified with additional alcohol. Sherries vary in color and sweetness.

Dry sherry is sold as fino (dry and light) or manzanilla (a very dry, slightly salty fino). Chefs keep dry sherry on hand because it adds great flavor to sauces and marinades. Amontillado is a **medium sherry**, nuttier and darker than the finos. The sweetest sherry is oloroso, which is also called **cream sherry**.

A natural with lamb, rosemary gives the marinade
in this dish a pleasantly woodsy touch

LAMB CHOPS WITH ROSEMARY AND GARLIC

Serves 6 ↣ Prep Time: 10 minutes ↣ Marinating Time: at least 6 hours
Grilling Time: 10 minutes; medium heat

INGREDIENTS

½ cup olive oil

½ cup dry red wine

1 tablespoon dried rosemary leaves, crushed or 3 tablespoons chopped fresh rosemary leaves

1½ tablespoons brown sugar

3 cloves garlic, minced

½ cup orange juice

12 double-cut rib lamb chops, trimmed of fat

Mint sauce or jelly, optional

1. COMBINE the olive oil, red wine, rosemary, brown sugar, garlic, and orange juice in a small bowl.

2. PLACE chops in a large glass baking dish. **POUR** marinade over them, **COVER** with plastic wrap, then **REFRIGERATE** for at least 6 hours, turning the chops once or twice.

3. BRUSH or spray the grill grid with vegetable oil. **PREHEAT** grill to medium.

4. REMOVE the chops from the dish and discard the marinade. Using tongs to turn the chops, **GRILL** for 4 to 5 minutes per side for medium rare.

5. REMOVE chops from grill and **SERVE** immediately, with mint sauce.

The advantage of asking your butcher for double-cut lamb
chops is twofold: The outside of the chops seals in the juices,
while the inside stays nicely pink. In summer, homegrown
zucchini and tomatoes make garden-fresh side dishes.

TERIYAKI LONDON BROIL

Serves 6 ➼ Prep Time: 15 minutes ➼ Marinating Time: 2 hours or more
Grilling Time: 12–14 minutes; medium-high heat

INGREDIENTS

½ cup ketchup

½ cup soy sauce

¼ cup Worcestershire sauce

1 tablespoon Dijon-style mustard

1 teaspoon powdered ginger or 1 tablespoon chopped fresh ginger; (see page 29)

3 cloves garlic, minced

1 large shallot, minced

Salt and pepper to taste

1 2½-pound sirloin steak (London broil)

1. In a medium bowl, **COMBINE** the ketchup, soy sauce, Worcestershire, mustard, ginger, garlic, shallot, salt, and pepper. **PLACE** steak in a resealable plastic bag. **POUR** in marinade and seal the bag, then **TURN** several times to coat steak.

2. Let steak **MARINATE** at room temperature for 2 hours (or in the refrigerator for up to 8 hours), turning the bag once or twice.

3. BRUSH or spray the grill grid with vegetable oil. **PREHEAT** the grill to medium-high.

4. GRILL steak for 1 minute on each side with lid up, then lower the lid and grill 5 to 6 minutes on each side for medium-rare or to desired doneness.

5. TRANSFER the steak to a cutting board and let rest for 5 minutes. Thinly **SLICE** on the diagonal and **SERVE** warm.

Ask the Experts

What is London Broil ?
Technically, London Broil is a large piece of flank steak (see page 129) that has been tenderized, then broiled or grilled and, finally, sliced thinly across the grain. The term has also come to be used for other thick cuts of meat, including top round and sirloin tip, when they're prepared in the same way.

What are shallots?
Shallots look like a cross between onions and garlic. Like garlic, shallots grow in a head made up of several cloves, yet the outer skin is similar to the color of a brown-skinned onion.

The shallot's flavor is more akin to that of a mild onion than to garlic, and the cloves are prized by cooks for their tender texture.

Dry shallots are sold year-round. Choose shallots with cloves that are plump and firm—no wrinkles, no sprouts.

Turn ordinary pork chops into a flavorful feast

CITRUS GRILLED PORK CHOPS

Serves 6 ❧ Prep Time: 20 minutes ❧ Marinating Time: 2 hours or more
Grilling Time: 12–14 minutes; medium-high heat

INGREDIENTS

3 tablespoons olive oil

4 cloves garlic, minced

1 large shallot, chopped

1½ teaspoons ground cumin

⅓ cup lime juice

½ cup orange juice

2 teaspoons salt

1 teaspoon pepper

1 teaspoon dried oregano

⅓ cup water

6 1-inch-thick pork chops

1. HEAT oil in a medium saucepan over medium heat. Add garlic and shallot, and **SAUTÉ** 1 to 2 minutes, stirring constantly.

2. STIR in the cumin, lime and orange juices, salt, pepper, oregano, and water. **COOK** for 5 minutes over medium-low heat. Remove from heat and let cool slightly.

3. ARRANGE the chops in a shallow glass or ceramic dish and pour half the sauce over them. (**REFRIGERATE** remaining sauce until ready to use.) **TURN** the chops to coat, cover with plastic wrap, and **REFRIGERATE** for at least 2 hours or overnight.

4. BRUSH or spray the grill grid with vegetable oil. **PREHEAT** the grill to medium-high.

5. GRILL the chops with the lid up for 1 minute on each side, then lower lid and grill for 5 to 6 minutes per side. **REMOVE** from the grill.

6. REHEAT sauce uncovered in microwave for 1 minute and **SPOON** over chops. **SERVE.**

Pork Cuts

The pork chop isn't the only part of the pig that tastes great grilled. Try **Pork loin** that is stuffed and rolled before grilling, then sliced into tasty pinwheels after it's done. Pork tenderloin (considerably cheaper than beef tenderloin but still delicious) is a long, cylindrical cut that takes better to indirect grilling. **Spare ribs** and the smaller but more tender **baby back ribs** are perennial stars of the backyard barbecue, whether smoked or grilled. Like pork tenderloin, baby back ribs require indirect grilling.

FIRST PERSON DISASTER

Out of Gas

My in-laws were coming for a barbecue on Sunday afternoon, and I really wanted to impress them with a grilled steak. Everything was all set, and I was proud of myself for being so organized for once!

When we were ready to grill, I sprayed the grill rack with vegetable spray like the recipe said and preheated the grill. After a few minutes, I looked at the temperature gauge on the lid and noticed that it had barely climbed to 200 degrees. What was wrong? I suddenly remembered that the last time we had used the grill, the gas tank had registered about one-third full. Could I possibly be out of gas?

Just then, I heard a slight puff and noticed that there was no gas in the burners. I turned off the grill and checked the gauge—the propane tank was empty, and my in-laws were waiting for their steaks. I didn't like the thought of finishing the steaks under the broiler, so I quickly pulled out our old charcoal grill, filled it with "quick -lite" charcoal, lit it, and waited a few minutes for the coals to burn down.

Somehow I managed to grill the steaks to perfection, and no one ever knew what had happened. It's always helpful to have a backup grill, but next time I'll check the gauge on the gas tank before my company arrives.

Fred K., Seattle, Washington

Choose veal chops that are at least an inch thick so that they'll keep their juiciness and delicate flavor when grilled

VEAL CHOPS WITH HERB BUTTER

Serves 6 ✦ Prep Time: 10 minutes ✦ Marinating Time: 4 hours or more
Grilling Time: 12–14 minutes; high heat

INGREDIENTS

4 tablespoons butter, room temperature

1 teaspoon dried basil or 1 tablespoon finely chopped fresh basil

1 teaspoon dried, crushed rosemary; or 1 tablespoon finely chopped fresh rosemary

6 loin veal chops, about 12 ounces each

4 to 5 tablespoons olive oil

1 medium shallot, minced

2 tablespoons lemon juice

Salt and pepper to taste

FOR THE HERB BUTTER

1. In a small bowl, **COMBINE** the butter and herbs. **BLEND** well.

2. COVER and refrigerate until ready to use.

FOR THE CHOPS

1. PLACE chops in a shallow glass dish. In a bowl, **COMBINE** the olive oil, shallot, lemon juice, salt, and pepper. **POUR** marinade over the veal chops and turn to coat both sides. Cover with plastic wrap and **MARINATE** in the refrigerator for 4 hours or overnight.

2. BRUSH or spray the grill grid with vegetable oil. **PREHEAT** the grill to high.

3. REMOVE the veal chops from the dish, reserving marinade. **GRILL** with lid up for 1 minute on each side, then lower lid and grill for 5 to 6 minutes on each side.

4. REMOVE the chops from the grill and transfer to a platter. **TOP** with Herb Butter and **SERVE** immediately.

A bit of the basil-flavored butter from these grilled veal chops
might also be good with grilled Marinated Portobello
Mushrooms (see page 82). The best quality veal is almost free
of fat and has a dense, fine texture and creamy white color.
But take note: The absence of fat causes the meat to become
dry if it spends too much time on the grill.

These are quick and delicious. If you aren't keen on spicy flavors, omit the hot red pepper sauce

TEQUILA PORK LOIN CHOPS

Serves 6 •• Prep Time: 12 minutes •• Grilling Time: 12 minutes; medium heat

INGREDIENTS

½ cup orange marmalade

2 tablespoons tequila

2 tablespoons lime juice

½ teaspoon hot red pepper sauce

½ teaspoon powdered ginger; or 2 teaspoons chopped fresh ginger

2 cloves garlic, minced

Salt and pepper to taste

6 boneless pork loin chops, cut 1-inch thick and trimmed

Pineapple–Red Pepper Salsa, optional (see opposite page)

1. COMBINE the marmalade, tequila, lime juice, red pepper sauce, ginger, garlic, salt, and pepper in a small bowl.

2. RUB marinade over both sides of chops and set aside.

3. BRUSH or spray the grill grid with vegetable oil. **PREHEAT** grill to medium.

4. GRILL chops with lid up for 1 minute on each side, then lower lid and grill for 5 minutes on each side.

5. REMOVE from grill and **SERVE** with Pineapple–Red Pepper Salsa if desired.

Pineapple-Red Pepper Salsa

1 16-ounce can crushed pineapple; or 2½ cups fresh pineapple, chopped

1 large red bell pepper, cored, seeded, and chopped

½ medium red onion, chopped

¼ cup lime juice

2 teaspoons dried chives or 1½ tablespoons snipped fresh chives or cilantro

Pepper to taste

1. COMBINE pineapple, red bell pepper, onion, lime juice, chives, and pepper in a medium bowl.

2. COVER and set aside until ready to serve.

Ask the Experts

My grilled pork chops always seem to turn out too dry. Why?

Today's leaner pork comes at the expense of juiciness, so don't blame yourself. Brining the chops before grilling—in other words, marinating them in salt water—will make the grilled chops moister.

Make the brine by adding 3 tablespoons coarse salt to 1 cup hot water; whisk until the salt is dissolved. Place the pork chops in a glass bowl or resealable plastic bag, then pour in the brine; let sit for 2 to 4 hours. Discard the brine and proceed with your recipe. (There's no need to rinse the chops before grilling.)

FIESTA GRILLED BEEF SALAD

Serves 6 ⇢ Prep Time: 30 minutes ⇢ Marinating Time: 1–2 hours
Grilling Time: 10–14 minutes; high heat

INGREDIENTS

6 cloves garlic, minced

2 teaspoons powdered ginger or 2 tablespoons minced fresh ginger

4 green onions (white and green parts), chopped

2 tablespoons honey

½ cup soy sauce

½ cup lime juice

⅓ cup orange juice

4 tablespoons sesame oil or olive oil

2 1¼-pound flank steaks

8 cups mesclun (mixed baby greens)

1 seedless cucumber, thinly sliced

1 medium red onion, thinly sliced

1 red or yellow bell pepper, cored, seeded, and thinly sliced

2 ripe avocados, peeled, pitted, and cut into slices

FOR THE BEEF

1. COMBINE the garlic, ginger, green onions, honey, soy sauce, lime and orange juices, and oil in a bowl. **RESERVE** ⅓ of the marinade.

2. PLACE the flank steaks in 2 resealable plastic bags, **POUR** in the marinade in equal parts, seal the bags, and **REFRIGERATE** 1 to 2 hours.

3. BRUSH or spray the grilling grid with vegetable oil. **PREHEAT** the grill to high heat.

4. REMOVE the flank steaks from the bags, discarding marinade. **GRILL** with lid up for 1 minute on each side, then lower lid and grill for 4 to 6 minutes on each side for medium rare or to desired doneness.

5. TRANSFER the steaks to a cutting board and let rest for 3 minutes. **CUT** into paper-thin slices on the diagonal, across the grain.

FOR THE SALAD

1. In a large salad bowl, **COMBINE** mesclun, cucumber, onion, pepper, and avocados. **TOSS** with enough of the reserved marinade to dress lightly, then divide evenly among 6 dinner plates.

2. TOP with the sliced steak and **SERVE** immediately.

Ask the Experts

How can I tell when the meat is done?

If you don't have a meat thermometer, try the novel "open-hand" method to test for doneness: Simply compare the resistance of the meat when you press it lightly to that of a particular part of your hand.

In general, cooked meat is **medium** when you press it and it feels like the fleshy part of your palm just below the lower thumb knuckle.

Rare has the same feel as the tissue between your thumb and the lowest knuckle of your index finger (right where your hand makes a U).

Meat that is **well done** feels like the base of your thumb—the part just above the wrist.

When should I use a meat thermometer?

For cuts that are thicker than 1 inch, you can use an instant-read thermometer. But remember that meat continues to cook once removed from the source of heat, so take that into account while the meat rests and the juices are settling. The thermometer should read 130°F for rare, 150°F for medium, and 170°F for well done.

SEAFOOD

Swordfish is one of the easiest cuts of fish to grill, and this marinade makes it fabulous! For added flavor, serve with salsa

SOUTH SEAS SWORDFISH

Serves 6 ‣‣ Prep Time: 10 minutes ‣‣ Marinating Time: 30 minutes to 3 hours
Grilling Time: 8–10 minutes; medium-high heat

INGREDIENTS

⅓ cup olive oil

⅓ cup lime juice

3 tablespoons pineapple juice

¼ cup dark rum

1 teaspoon ground ginger or 1 tablespoon fresh grated ginger (see page 29)

2 cloves garlic, minced

½ teaspoon pepper

6 1-inch-thick swordfish steaks, about 6 to 8 ounces each

Fruit Salsa, optional (see opposite page)

I. In a medium bowl, **WHISK** together the olive oil, lime and pineapple juices, rum, ginger, garlic, and pepper.

2. PLACE swordfish steaks in glass or ceramic dish and **POUR** the marinade over them. **TURN** steaks to coat evenly. Cover, place in the refrigerator, and **MARINATE** for up to 3 hours, turning the steaks once.

3. BRUSH or spray the grill grid with vegetable oil. **PREHEAT** grill to medium-high.

4. REMOVE swordfish from the dish, discarding marinade. **GRILL** with lid open for 1 minute on each side, then lower the lid and grill the steaks 3 to 4 minutes on each side or until they begin to turn opaque in the center (see opposite page).

5. REMOVE swordfish from grill and **SERVE** with Fruit Salsa, if desired.

TIPS · AND · TECHNIQUES

Buying Swordfish

Swordfish—at 600 to 1000 pounds, one of the biggest catches in the sea—is popular because its mild, firm flesh can be prepared so many ways, from grilling to baking to sautéing. It is sold fresh or frozen, as either steaks or chunks. Fresh is best and is available from late spring to early fall.

FRUIT SALSA

1 cup diced cantaloupe

½ cup diced pineapple

½ cup diced peaches or nectarines

2 tablespoons chopped red or green onion (white and green parts)

1 teaspoon chopped canned jalapeños (optional)

1½ tablespoons fresh chopped basil and/or mint

2 teaspoons fresh lime juice

1. COMBINE all ingredients in a medium bowl.

2. Cover and **CHILL**, then bring the salsa to room temperature before serving.

Ask the Experts

My grilled swordfish turned out dry and chewy. Did I do something wrong?
Most likely you overcooked the fish. To check for doneness, work the tip of a knife between the layers of flesh at the steak's edge and take a peek. If the interior is starting to turn opaque or if it registers 140°F on an instant-read thermometer, the fish is done.

Swordfish and this spicy, sweet sauce are a delicious match

SWORDFISH KEBABS WITH RED PEPPER SAUCE

Serves 6 ◆◆ Prep Time: 15–20 minutes ◆◆ Marinating Time: 30 minutes
Grilling Time: 8–10 minutes; medium-high heat

INGREDIENTS

3 tablespoons olive oil

3 tablespoons lemon or lime juice

1 teaspoon chili powder

2 teaspoons paprika

1/2 teaspoon ground cumin

1 teaspoon salt

2 pounds swordfish steaks, skin removed, cut into 1 1/2-inch cubes

12 metal skewers

Red Pepper Sauce (see opposite page)

1. In a medium bowl, **COMBINE** the olive oil, lemon juice, chili powder, paprika, cumin, and salt.

2. ADD the swordfish and turn to coat thoroughly. Cover, then transfer to the refrigerator and **MARINATE** for 30 minutes.

3. THREAD the swordfish onto skewers.

4. BRUSH or spray the grill grid with vegetable oil. **PREHEAT** grill to medium-high.

5. GRILL the fish with the lid up for about 5 minutes, turning occasionally, or until fish is just opaque (see page 145).

6. SERVE warm with Red Pepper Sauce (see opposite page).

RED PEPPER SAUCE

1 14-ounce jar roasted peppers, drained; or 2 whole red peppers, roasted (see directions on this page)

4 cloves garlic, finely chopped

4 tablespoons lemon juice

1/2 cup mayonnaise

1/2 teaspoon each salt and pepper

1. COMBINE the peppers, garlic, lemon juice, mayonnaise, salt, and pepper in a blender or food processor fitted with a steel blade.

2. PUREE until smooth. Cover and **CHILL** until ready to serve. Sauce is best served at room temperature.

Ask the Experts

How do I roast whole peppers on the grill?

To roast the red peppers, just follow the steps below. Alternatively, you can place peppers under a broiler before proceeding with steps 3 and 4.

1. PREHEAT the grill to medium-high.

2. GRILL the peppers, turning often, for about 10 to 12 minutes or until the skin is black and blistered.

3. PLACE peppers in a paper bag, seal completely, and let the peppers steam for 15 minutes.

4. REMOVE peppers from the bag, then remove and discard blackened skin and the stems and seeds.

I don't want to fuss with kebabs. Can I use this recipe for swordfish steaks?

Sure you can. You'll need about 5 to 8 ounces per person, so buy two swordfish steaks that weigh about a pound each. The marinade and grilling directions are the same as for the kebabs. When you're done grilling, simply cut the steaks into thirds and serve. You'll have enough for 6.

This marinade helps ensure that
the tuna doesn't dry out during grilling

ASIAN TUNA STEAKS

Serves 6 ⇥ Prep Time: 15 minutes ⇥ Marinating Time: 1 hour
Grilling Time: 6–8 minutes; high heat

INGREDIENTS

1/4 cup sesame or olive oil

1/4 cup soy sauce

2 tablespoons orange juice

1 tablespoon honey

3 cloves garlic, minced

2 teaspoons ground ginger or 2 tablespoons chopped fresh ginger (see page 29)

1/2 teaspoon pepper

6 6-ounce tuna steaks, about 1 1/2 -inches thick

1. In a small bowl, **WHISK** together the oil, soy sauce, orange juice, honey, garlic, ginger, and pepper.

2. PLACE tuna steaks in a resealable plastic bag and **POUR** marinade over steaks. Seal the bag, then **TURN** to coat. **MARINATE** in the refrigerator for 1 hour.

3. BRUSH or spray the grill grid with vegetable oil. **PREHEAT** grill to high.

4. REMOVE tuna from the bag, discarding the marinade.

5. GRILL steaks with lid down for 3 to 4 minutes on each side for rare to medium-rare. **REMOVE** from the grill and **SERVE** warm.

Grill marks on a tuna steak, served here with wild rice, make this hearty
fish seem all the meatier. If you like it rare in the center, take extra care to
buy the highest quality tuna, and the freshest you can find.

No marinating needed—simply brush on this delectable glaze, then grill

SALMON WITH MUSTARD GLAZE

Serves 6 ⟶ Prep Time: 10–15 minutes ⟶ Grilling Time: 12 minutes; medium heat

INGREDIENTS

2 tablespoons brown sugar

1 tablespoon honey

2 tablespoons Dijon-style mustard

2 tablespoons soy sauce

3 tablespoons white wine or dry sherry

2 tablespoons olive oil

2 teaspoons ground ginger or 1½ tablespoons grated fresh ginger (see page 29)

6 6-ounce salmon fillets, with skin (see opposite page)

1. COMBINE brown sugar, honey, mustard, soy sauce, wine, olive oil, and ginger in a small saucepan over low heat for 2 to 3 minutes or until sugar is melted and ingredients are combined.

2. REMOVE from heat and set aside.

3. BRUSH or spray the grill grid with vegetable oil. **PREHEAT** grill to medium heat.

4. PLACE salmon skin-side down on the grill. **BRUSH** the tops of the fish with the glaze.

5. GRILL with lid down for 10 to 12 minutes or until fish is just cooked through (the skin will appear dark and crisp).

6. SLIDE a spatula between the skin and flesh, and lift the fish, leaving the skin behind. (Remove skin after the grill has cooled.) **SERVE** the salmon warm.

Ask the Experts

Why is salmon supposed to be so good for me?

Salmon is one of the richest sources of omega-3 fatty acids—"good" fats in every sense of the word. One of the two types of polyunsaturated fats, omega 3 is believed to lower blood cholesterol and triglycerides, thus helping ward off cardiovascular disease. Because our bodies don't produce polyunsatured fatty acids, we need to ingest about 1 to 3 grams per day—and a 5-ounce salmon steak provides 2.7 grams!

Other oily fish rich in omega-3 fatty acids include mackerel, herring, anchovies, and albacore and bluefin tunas. Shrimp and other shellfish also supply plenty of helpful omega 3s.

Buying Salmon

Fresh salmon is widely available and is sold either whole or cut into steaks or fillets. **Salmon steak** is horseshoe-shaped and thick, and has black skin around the sides. A **salmon fillet** is much thinner, has no real edge, and has skin on one side (fillets are the cut used for smoked salmon). When shopping for salmon, buy the freshest possible, preferably from a fish market with a lot of turnover.

FIRST PERSON DISASTER

Stuck Like Glue

My fish was marinating and everything was all set for dinner, except that it looked like it was going to rain. When I dashed out to preheat the gas grill, it was pouring. In my haste to get out of the rain, I forgot to oil the grill. By the time I got the fillets on the hot grill grid, there was a clap of thunder. Back inside I went.

When I went out a few minutes later, I couldn't slide the spatula underneath the fish to turn it. The fish was stuck to the grid—I mean REALLY stuck. I managed to leave the burned part of the fillet on the grill, scooping up the remains to salvage about half of each one.

What had I done wrong? I suddenly remembered that I hadn't sprayed the grid with vegetable oil, as the recipe had indicated. Next time, I'll cover all my bases so that my fish won't stick! And I'll try not to grill in the rain.

Jaye W., Canton, Ohio

Tuna steaks marinated in rum and lime—fabulous!

MARINATED TUNA STEAKS

Serves 6 ◆ Prep Time: 15 minutes ◆ Marinating Time: 30 minutes to 1 hour
Grilling Time: 6–8 minutes; medium-high heat

INGREDIENTS

¼ cup olive oil

¼ cup lime juice

2 tablespoons dark rum

2 tablespoons soy sauce

½ teaspoon salt

¼ teaspoon pepper

6 6- to 8-ounce tuna steaks, each about ¾-inch thick

1. In a small bowl, **WHISK** together the oil, lime juice, rum, soy sauce, salt, and pepper.

2. PLACE tuna in a large resealable plastic bag and **POUR** mixture into bag. Seal bag, then **TURN** to coat fish. **MARINATE** in the refrigerator for up to 1 hour.

3. BRUSH or spray the grill grid with vegetable oil. **PREHEAT** grill to medium-high.

4. REMOVE tuna from the bag, discarding the marinade.

5. GRILL with lid up for 1 minute on each side, then lower lid and grill for 2 to 3 minutes on each side for rare.

6. REMOVE from grill and **SERVE**.

Types of Tuna

Tuna comes in a range of sizes, colors, and tastes. The most delicate species, and that of prime interest to canneries, is **albacore**. This small tuna is the only one labeled "white-meat tuna" by U.S. regulations. Like albacore, the tuna called **bonito** is small, but it's hardly the same quality.

The main Atlantic tuna species is **bluefin**, which can weigh up to 1,000 pounds. It has deep-red flesh and is more strongly flavored than albacore. **Yellowfin**, a Pacific tuna whose flesh has a light pink tone, is smaller in size and has a very delicate flavor. Not surprisingly, yellowfin is prized by chefs.

Albacore Tuna

This simple sauce is great served with any white fish fillet—so give it a try with sole, cod, or grouper

GRILLED HALIBUT WITH LEMON-BASIL SAUCE

Serves 6 ▸▸ Prep Time: 10 minutes ▸▸ Grilling Time: 8 minutes; medium-high heat

INGREDIENTS

4 tablespoons olive oil

5 tablespoons lemon juice

4 cloves garlic, minced

2 tablespoons dried basil or 6 tablespoons thinly sliced fresh basil

1/4 cup oil-packed sun-dried tomatoes, finely chopped (see page 53)

1 teaspoon sugar

1/2 teaspoon salt

1/4 teaspoon pepper or hot red pepper flakes

6 6-ounce halibut steaks, each about 3/4-inch thick

1. WHISK together the oil, lemon juice, garlic, basil, sun-dried tomatoes, sugar, salt, and pepper in a small saucepan over medium heat. **COOK,** stirring, 1 to 2 minutes or until the sugar dissolves. **REMOVE** from heat and set aside.

2. BRUSH or spray the grill grid with vegetable oil. **PREHEAT** grill to medium-high.

3. DIVIDE the sauce in half. **BRUSH** both sides of the halibut steaks with half of the sauce, reserving the other half. **GRILL** fish with the lid up for 4 minutes on each side or until opaque.

4. TRANSFER fish to plates and **SPOON** the reserved sauce over each steak. **SERVE** warm.

Though its firm white flesh is mild-tasting, halibut holds up to a savory sauce of sun-dried tomatoes with basil and lemon. Fish cools rapidly, so it's a good idea to warm your serving or dinner plates in the oven.

This sweet-and-sour sauce turns grilled scallops
and shrimp into a taste-bud-tingling seafood feast

TERIYAKI SEAFOOD-VEGETABLE KEBABS

Serves 6 ▸▸ Prep Time: 20 minutes ▸▸ Grilling Time: 4 minutes; medium-high heat

INGREDIENTS

½ cup soy sauce

4 tablespoons brown sugar

½ cup dry sherry

¼ cup orange juice

¼ cup sesame or olive oil

2 teaspoons ground ginger or 2 tablespoons minced fresh ginger (see page 29)

¼ teaspoon dried red pepper flakes or to taste

4 cloves garlic, minced

24 sea scallops

24 jumbo shrimp, peeled and deveined (see page 31)

24 medium mushrooms, cut in half

6 red bell peppers, cut into 36 pieces, each 1-inch square

3 onions cut into ½-inch wedges

12 12-inch skewers (see page 23)

I. COMBINE the soy sauce, brown sugar, sherry, orange juice, sesame oil, ginger, red pepper flakes, and garlic in a small saucepan over medium-high heat. Bring to a boil, reduce heat to low, and **SIMMER** for 1 minute, stirring. **REMOVE** from heat and set aside.

2. THREAD 2 scallops, 2 shrimp, 4 mushroom halves, 3 pieces of red pepper, and 3 onion slices onto each skewer.

3. BRUSH kebabs with glaze and set aside.

4. BRUSH or spray the grill grid with vegetable oil. **PREHEAT** grill to medium-high.

5. GRILL kebabs with lid up for 2 minutes on each side or until shrimp are pink and scallops are just opaque.

6. Using an oven mitt, **REMOVE** kebabs from grill. **SERVE** immediately.

TIPS AND TECHNIQUES

Ask the Experts

How long does fresh fish keep in the refrigerator?
Fresh fish should be cooked no more than a day or two after purchase. When you buy fresh fish, wrap it tightly in plastic wrap and refrigerate it immediately. Remove fish from the refrigerator 30 minutes before cooking.

Buying Scallops

There are two types of scallops: The **sea scallop** is about $1^{1}/_{2}$ inches in diameter, while the **bay scallop,** at about $^{1}/_{2}$ inch, supports the supposition that smaller is better by being sweeter and more succulent.

Fresh sea scallops are in their peak season from October to April, fresh bay scallops in fall. Both kinds, which are usually sold shucked (out of the shell), range in color from pale beige to ivory pink and should have a sweet smell and a moist sheen. (Beware of scallops that are pure white—it's a clue they've been soaked in water to plump them up.)

Refrigerate scallops as quickly as you can after purchasing, and prepare them within two days.

These shrimp are wonderful served at
room temperature over a bed of leafy greens

SHRIMP WITH DILL

Serves 6 ◆◆ Prep Time: 20 minutes ◆◆ Marinating Time: 1 hour
Grilling Time: 4–6 minutes; high heat

INGREDIENTS

2½ pounds extra-large
shrimp, peeled and
deveined (see page 31)

½ cup lemon juice

½ cup olive oil

3 tablespoons dried dill
weed or ⅓ cup fresh
chopped dill

1. PEEL and **DEVEIN** shrimp, then set aside.

2. COMBINE lemon juice, olive oil, and dill in a large resealable
plastic bag. **ADD** the shrimp, seal the bag, and **TOSS** to coat.
MARINATE in the refrigerator for 1 hour.

3. BRUSH or spray a perforated grill pan (see page 76) with
vegetable oil. Place shrimp in grill pan. **PREHEAT** grill to high.

4. GRILL shrimp in pan with grill lid up for 2 minutes on
each side.

5. REMOVE from grill and **SERVE**.

Buying Shrimp

These tasty little crustaceans range in size from small to jumbo, and though the varieties are slightly different in taste and texture, all but the smallest can usually take another's place in a recipe.

Shrimp are sold year-round, usually without the head; the legs, too, are often removed. You can choose raw or cooked, shelled or unshelled, and fresh or frozen shrimp. If **raw shrimp** doesn't smell of the sea (and if it has any hint of ammonia), pass it by. When buying **cooked shelled shrimp,** choose fresh-smelling shrimp that are also nice and plump.

Ask the Experts

How long can I store fresh uncooked shrimp?
Two days is the limit. Cooked shrimp can be stored in the fridge for up to 3 days.

What's the best way to thaw frozen shrimp?
Frozen shrimp will keep for up to 3 months. You can either thaw them in their freezer wrapping overnight in the fridge or place the package in cold water until the shrimp have defrosted. Never refreeze seafood once it's been thawed.

How Many Shrimp in a Pound?

Size	Raw in the shell per pound	Peeled per pound	Cooked per pound
Jumbo	21–25	26–30	31–35
Large	31–40	36–45	41–50
Medium	41–50	46–55	51–60
Small	51–60	56–65	61–70

*A flavorful breadcrumb coating turns these
grilled scallops into a fabulous meal*

SCALLOPS ITALIANO

Serves 6 ◆◆ Prep Time: 15 minutes ◆◆ Marinating Time: 30 minutes to 1 hour
Grilling Time: 4–6 minutes; high heat

INGREDIENTS

1/3 cup dried bread-
crumbs

1/3 cup grated Parmesan
cheese

1 teaspoon dried oregano

1/2 teaspoon each salt
and pepper

30 large sea scallops,
about 2 1/2 pounds, rinsed

3 tablespoons olive oil

Lemon-Garlic Topping,
optional (see box)

1. In a medium bowl, **COMBINE** breadcrumbs, Parmesan cheese, oregano, salt, and pepper. Set aside.

2. RINSE scallops under cold water and pat dry with paper towels. Place scallops on a plate, then **BRUSH** with olive oil.

3. DIP scallops in coating mixture and gently press the breadcrumbs onto all sides. **TRANSFER** the coated scallops to a plate, cover, and **REFRIGERATE** for up to 1 hour.

4. PREPARE optional topping (see below) and **RESERVE**.

5. PREHEAT grill to high.

6. PLACE scallops in a perforated grill pan (see page 76), and **GRILL** with lid up for 2 to 3 minutes on each side or until just opaque. Take care not to overcook.

7. REMOVE from grill and add even more flavor by sprinkling with Lemon-Garlic Topping. **SERVE.**

Lemon-Garlic Topping

2/3 cup chopped parsley
or 2 tablespoons dried parsley

3 tablespoons olive oil

3 tablespoons lemon juice

3 cloves garlic, minced

COMBINE ingredients in a bowl.

Set aside and refrigerate until ready to use.

Sea scallops are larger and more widely available than bay scallops. They are also a little chewier, but their meat is just as sweet and moist. Remembering which is which is easy: Just as with bodies of water, a sea is larger than a bay.

GRILLED LOBSTER TAILS

Serves 6 ▸▸ Prep Time: 10 minutes ▸▸ Marinating Time: 30 minutes
Grilling Time: 8–11 minutes; high heat

INGREDIENTS

6 spiny lobster tails, about 8 ounces each, split (see opposite page)

3 cloves garlic, minced

1/3 cup lemon juice

Salt and pepper to taste

1/2 cup butter (1 stick)

3 cloves garlic, minced

2 teaspoons dried thyme or 2 tablespoons chopped fresh thyme

1. PLACE split lobster tails shell-side down on a large platter, then **SPRINKLE** with garlic, lemon juice, salt, and pepper. Cover with plastic wrap and **REFRIGERATE** for 30 minutes.

2. MELT the butter in a small saucepan over low heat. **ADD** the garlic and thyme, then **COOK** for 2 minutes, stirring. Keep the mixture warm until ready to use.

3. BRUSH or spray the grill grid with vegetable oil. **PREHEAT** grill to high.

4. BRUSH the cut fleshy side of the lobster tails with some of the butter. Place tails cut-side down on grill grid and **GRILL** with lid down for 3 minutes.

5. Using tongs, **TURN** tails and **BRUSH** meat with more butter. **COOK** 5 to 8 minutes or until meat is white and slightly firm to the touch. Continue brushing tails with butter as they cook.

6. REMOVE lobster tails from grill and **SERVE**.

TIPS AND TECHNIQUES

Buying Lobster Tails

Succulent tail meat is the spiny lobster's claim to fame. Its tail not only is wider than that of a Maine lobster, but it has firm, sweet white meat that has been described as "lobster with a hint of shrimp." The tails most often are sold frozen outside of Florida and Southern California, whose waters the lobster calls home.

When buying spiny lobster tails, ask your fishmonger to split them for you, as in this recipe. Exposing the meat to the fire will enhance the flavor, as will basting the meat with butter.

Ask the Experts

How do I split a lobster tail?
To butterfly or split a lobster tail, use kitchen shears to cut through the top of the shell. Then cut the tail meat in half lengthwise, being careful not to slice through the bottom shell. When you open up the lobster tail, it should look like a butterfly.

Are spiny and rock lobsters the same thing?
Yes. And to add to the confusion, this small-clawed, spiny-shelled species also goes by the name of Florida lobster and langouste. Besides being found in the waters off Florida and California, spiny lobsters are trapped in New Zealand, Australia, Mexico, and South Africa.

Some commercial suppliers refer to the lobster itself as "spiny lobster" and call the frozen or canned tail meat rock lobster.

A treat for the adventurous, these sweet crustaceans are in season from May through August

GRILLED SOFT-SHELL CRABS

Serves 6 ◆◆ Prep Time: 10 minutes ◆◆ Marinating Time: 1 hour
Grilling Time: 4–8 minutes; high heat

INGREDIENTS

1½ sticks butter

3 small shallots, minced

3 cloves garlic, minced

2 teaspoons seafood seasoning, such as Old Bay

1 tablespoon lime juice

Salt and pepper to taste

6 soft-shell crabs, cleaned (see opposite page)

Tartar sauce (for homemade, see opposite page)

1. BRUSH or spray the grill grid with vegetable oil. Then **PREHEAT** the grill to high.

2. MELT butter with shallots, garlic, seafood seasoning, lime juice, salt, and pepper in a small saucepan over low heat. **COOK** for about 2 minutes (do not let the garlic brown). Remove from heat and **BRUSH** crabs generously with the butter mixture.

3. GRILL crabs with lid up for 2 to 4 minutes per side. **TURN** several times, until crabs are bright red all over and slightly charred in spots.

4. REMOVE crabs from grill and **SERVE** with tartar sauce.

HOMEMADE TARTAR SAUCE

1 cup mayonnaise

1 tablespoon drained capers, chopped

1 tablespoon minced dill pickles

1 tablespoon chopped fresh chives

1 tablespoon lime juice

1 tablespoon Dijon mustard

$\frac{1}{2}$ teaspoon pepper

1. COMBINE all ingredients in a small bowl.

2. COVER and **REFRIGERATE** until ready to serve.

Ask the Experts

What's a soft-shell crab?
A soft-shell crab is merely a blue crab that has just shed its shell, as crabs do periodically as they grow.

Cleaning these little creatures is not for everyone, so it's a good idea to ask your fishmonger to relieve you of the task. Soft-shell crabs should be cooked the same day you buy them.

Which other sauces besides tartar sauce go well with soft-shell crabs?
Any mayonnaise-based sauce will complement the crabs nicely, and you can be as creative as you like. For a taste of France, stir a tablespoon of chopped fresh basil and about half a tablespoon of fresh tarragon into a cup of mayonnaise.

Spicier flavors go well with crab, too: Add a couple of drops of hot red pepper sauce to the mayonnaise, then stir in a tablespoon or so of finely chopped chives. Taste, then add more hot sauce to raise the heat level, if you wish. Just don't make the finished sauce so hot that it overpowers the crab.

SANDWICHES

This is simple to prepare, but delicious!
If you prefer, substitute grilled zucchini

GRILLED EGGPLANT SANDWICHES

Serves 6 ◆◆ Prep Time: 15 minutes ◆◆ Grilling Time: 4–6 minutes; high heat

INGREDIENTS

1/3 cup olive oil

2 cloves garlic, minced

Salt and pepper to taste

2 medium eggplants, sliced lengthwise into 1/4-inch slices

6 6-inch-long whole-grain baguette-style rolls, sliced lengthwise

1/2 cup basil pesto (see page 117)

2 ripe tomatoes, cored and thinly sliced

12 ounces mozzarella cheese, sliced into 1/4-inch rounds

1. PREHEAT grill to high.

2. In a small bowl, **COMBINE** olive oil, garlic, salt, and pepper, and **WHISK** thoroughly.

3. BRUSH both sides of the eggplant slices with the olive oil mixture, coating evenly.

4. GRILL eggplant slices for 2 to 3 minutes on each side, or until tender but not mushy.

5. SPREAD cut sides of each roll with some of the pesto, then **TOP** with slices of eggplant, tomato, and cheese. **SERVE** warm or at room temperature.

Mozzarella Cheese

Mozzarella is more than just a pizza topping that melts well. Another plus for this snowy white, mild-tasting Italian specialty is its low fat content.

Of the cheese's two types—fresh and regular—fresh wins hands down. **Fresh mozzarella** is made from whole milk, is soft textured, and has a sweet, delicate taste; it usually comes packaged in whey or water. The choicest of the fresh mozzarellas is **buffalo mozzarella,** traditionally made from the milk of the water buffalo; today, it is more commonly made from cows' milk mixed with buffalos' milk.

Regular mozzarella, sold packaged in supermarkets, is drier and more rubbery than fresh, but it melts well, and is available in low-fat or nonfat varieties.

What's a Baguette?

Baguettes are long (usually 2 feet), slender loaves of French bread with a crisp brown crust. The interior is light and chewy, although it can quickly become dry—so the fresher the baguette, the better. Baguette rolls are 6 inches long.

This is really just a good ol' grilled ham-and-cheese sandwich—but flattened, Cuban-style!

GRILLED CUBAN SANDWICHES

Serves 6 ❧ Prep Time: 10 minutes ❧ Grilling Time: 4 minutes; medium heat

INGREDIENTS

12 1-inch thick slices of round peasant bread

Olive oil, for brushing bread

4 tablespoons Dijon-style mustard

18 slices Swiss or mozzarella cheese

18 slices baked ham

Salt and pepper to taste

1. BRUSH one side of each of the slices of bread with olive oil. Turn oil-side down on work surface covered with aluminum foil or wax paper.

2. SPREAD mustard on unoiled side of each of the slices of bread.

3. TOP 6 of the slices with 3 slices of cheese and 3 slices of ham. Add salt and pepper.

4. TOP each of the layered slices with a slice of bread oil-side up.

5. PREHEAT the grill to medium.

6. TRANSFER sandwiches to a perforated vegetable pan (see page 76). Weigh down sandwiches with a heavy skillet and **GRILL** for 2 minutes. Remove skillet and **TURN** sandwiches. Replace skillet on top of sandwiches, and grill for another 2 minutes or until nicely brown. Remove from grill and **SERVE** warm.

The pickles served with a Cuban sandwich are traditionally
sliced and placed between the layers of meat and cheese.
For another authentic touch, you can use Cuban bread,
if you're able to find it where you live. Before baking,
the dough of Cuban bread is scored across the top, and
bay leaves are nestled in the slits.

This herbed sandwich is great for a get-together with friends

GRILLED HERBED CHICKEN SANDWICHES

Serves 6 ◆▸ Prep Time: 8 minutes ◆▸ Marinating Time: at least 2 hours
Grilling Time: 8–10 minutes; high heat

INGREDIENTS

¾ cup lemon juice
(about 4 lemons)

¾ cup olive oil

1½ teaspoons salt

1 teaspoon pepper

½ teaspoon dried thyme

½ teaspoon dried basil

6 boneless, skinless
chicken breast halves,
rinsed and patted dry

1 cup mayonnaise or
Herb Mayonnaise (see
opposite page)

6 pieces of dense flat
Italian bread, sliced in
half horizontally

1 red onion, thinly sliced

2 cups torn arugula or
romaine lettuce, washed
and dried

1. In a small bowl, **WHISK** together the lemon juice, olive oil, salt, pepper, thyme, and basil. **POUR** into a resealable plastic bag. **ADD** the chicken, seal bag, and **MARINATE** in the refrigerator for at least 2 hours or overnight.

2. BRUSH or spray grill grid with vegetable oil. **PREHEAT** grill to high.

3. REMOVE chicken from the bag, discarding the marinade. **GRILL** chicken for 4 to 5 minutes on each side or until juices run clear when meat is pierced with the tip of a sharp knife. **REMOVE** chicken from the grill and keep warm.

4. SPREAD some mayonnaise over cut sides of each slice of bread. **TOP** with cooked chicken breast, slices of red onion, and arugula. **COVER** with top halves of bread, and cut sandwiches in half. **SERVE** immediately.

TIPS AND TECHNIQUES

Ask the Experts

Is making my own mayonnaise really worth the trouble?

Mayonnaise lovers swear by homemade, saying the flavor of store-bought just can't compare. The good news is that you don't have to be an experienced cook to make homemade mayonnaise. All you need is a blender or food processor, an egg, a large lemon, some oil, and salt and pepper.

Break the egg, squeeze 2 tablespoons of juice from the lemon, and pour $1/4$ cup canola or extra-virgin olive oil into a measuring cup. Combine all ingredients in the blender, adding salt and pepper to taste. Put another $3/4$ cup of oil in the measuring cup.

Turn on the blender, and add the oil in a thin, steady stream as the machine is running. When the mixture starts to thicken (usually after you've added about half the oil), you can add the oil a little faster.

To test the mayonnaise for thickness, taste a bit. If it needs thinning, add a little warm water while the blender is still running.

For extra flavor, stir in a pinch of dry mustard, cayenne pepper, or both.

Herb Mayonnaise

1 cup mayonnaise

1 tablespoon dried basil or $1/4$ cup chopped fresh basil

1 tablespoon dried thyme or $1/4$ cup chopped fresh thyme

$1^{1}/_{2}$ tablespoons lemon juice

1 clove garlic, minced

$1/2$ teaspoon pepper

1 teaspoon olive oil

1. In a small mixing bowl, **COMBINE** the mayonnaise, basil, thyme, lemon juice, garlic, pepper, and oil.

2. Cover and **REFRIGERATE** until ready to use.

This sandwich pairs the flavors of a grilled
cheese sandwich and a Greek salad

MEDITERRANEAN GRILLED CHEESE SANDWICHES

Serves 6 ◆◆ Prep Time: 15 minutes ◆◆ Grilling Time: 6–8 minutes; medium heat

INGREDIENTS

2 round loaves of crusty French or Italian bread (about 8 inches in diameter)

2/3 cup olive oil

1½ pounds feta cheese, cut into ¼-inch-thick slices

3 large tomatoes, cut in ¼-inch-thick slices

18 sun-dried tomatoes, either drained, if packed in oil, or rehydrated, then chopped (see page 53)

1 tablespoon dried oregano or 3 tablespoons finely chopped fresh oregano

Pepper to taste

1. TRIM and discard the ends of the bread loaves, then **SLICE** each loaf into 6 ½-inch-thick slices. When you are done, you should have 12 slices. **BRUSH** both sides of each slice with a little olive oil.

2. PREHEAT grill to medium and **PLACE** bread slices on the grill grid. **COOK** on one side for 2 to 3 minutes or until the bread is lightly toasted. Using tongs, **REMOVE** the bread from the grill and lay on work surface, grilled-side up.

3. ARRANGE 2 slices each of the feta cheese and tomato on 6 of the bread slices. **TOP** each with sun-dried tomatoes, then **SPRINKLE** with chopped oregano and pepper.

4. TOP with another slice of bread, ungrilled-side up. Place the sandwiches on grill and **COOK** for 2 minutes on each side or until golden. **REMOVE** from grill and cut each sandwich in half, if desired. **SERVE** immediately.

Variations on a Classic

A grilled cheese sandwich can be adapted to virtually any type of cuisine. Just omit the sun-dried tomatoes, substitute a different cheese for the feta, and vary the herb.

For a south-of-the-border variation, use jalapeño-flavored Monterey Jack cheese, and cumin in place of the oregano.

A grilled Swiss cheese sandwich could be topped with sautéed onions, then sprinkled with chopped parsley.

FIRST PERSON   DISASTER

Rock Hard

My kids wanted something different for dinner last night, so I suggested making some sandwiches on the grill. This was a novelty for them and a fun distraction from homework, but little did I know how much grief I'd take for this one!

I bought a delicious, dense loaf of country bread at the bakery that I knew would be great on the grill. Then each of us stuffed various goodies like ham, cheese, and vegetables between the bread slices, and I flattened the sandwiches with a large iron frying pan, just as the recipe said.

Then onto the grill. After a little while, I noticed that the grill didn't seem very hot. Was it out of gas? Probably so, but I figured that if I left the sandwiches on the warm grill, the cheese would melt and the bread would eventually toast.

Well, I was right on one count but way off base on the other. After what seemed like hours, I took the sandwiches off the grill. They didn't look too bad, and the cheese was oozing all over the place. But when I took a knife to the bread, it was as hard as a rock! I'd forgotten to brush both sides of the bread with oil, and leaving the sandwiches on the grill for so long hardened them to the point of no return. If it takes more than 3 minutes to toast, then it's called baking.

Maya T., Cleveland, Ohio

This moist and tender sandwich has
a marvelous mix of flavors

GRILLED SALMON SANDWICHES WITH PINEAPPLE

Serves 6 ⇢ Prep Time: 20 minutes ⇢ Marinating Time: 2 hours
Grilling Time: 10–12 minutes; medium-high heat

INGREDIENTS

5 tablespoons olive oil

1 tablespoon lime juice

1 teaspoon dried basil or
1 tablespoon minced
fresh basil

Salt and pepper to taste

6 6-ounce skinless
salmon fillets, about
3/4-inch thick

2 round loaves of crusty
peasant bread, cut into
1/2-inch-thick slices

6 slices pineapple

1/2 cup mayonnaise or
Herb Mayonnaise (see
page 173)

6 slices tomato

6 slices red onion

Lettuce leaves

1. COMBINE the oil, lime juice, basil, salt, and pepper in a large glass baking dish. Add salmon and **TURN** to coat both sides. Cover and **REFRIGERATE** for up to 2 hours.

2. BRUSH or spray a perforated vegetable pan with vegetable oil and place directly on grill grid. **PREHEAT** grill to medium-high.

3. PLACE salmon in the pan, and **GRILL** for 3 to 4 minutes on each side or until just opaque.

4. While the salmon is cooking, **GRILL** the bread and pineapple slices for 2 minutes on each side (grill the bread until golden-brown, the pineapple until slightly charred).

5. REMOVE fish, bread, and pineapple from grill. **SPREAD** 2 tablespoons of mayonnaise mixture over half the bread slices. **TOP** half the slices with pineapple, tomato, and red onion slices, then with a lettuce leaf and salmon fillet. **COVER** with remaining slices of bread and **CUT** each sandwich in half. **SERVE** warm.

Canned pineapple slices are just fine as a sweet, crunchy topping for salmon, but fresh ones are even better. To slice a fresh pineapple, use a very sharp knife. Slice off the leafy top, then slice the pineapple into rounds about ⅓-inch thick. Use a paring knife to remove the skin from each slice and to carve out the woody core.

This twist on a traditional Middle Eastern
dish is served rather like a taco

GRILLED LAMB
PITA SANDWICHES

Serves 6 ❧ Prep Time: 20 minutes ❧ Refrigeration Time: 2 hours
Grilling Time: 12 minutes; medium-high heat

INGREDIENTS

1½ pounds ground lamb

1 bunch green onions
(white and green parts),
finely minced

½ cup chopped fresh
parsley

2 tablespoons water

1 tablespoon lemon juice

1 tablespoon ground
cinnamon

1 teaspoon ground cumin

1½ teaspoons allspice

½ teaspoon each salt
and pepper

6 pita-bread rounds

1½ cups prepared
hummus

1. In a medium bowl, **COMBINE** the ground lamb, green onions, parsley, water, lemon juice, cinnamon, cumin, allspice, salt, and pepper. **MIX** thoroughly. **DIVIDE** mixture into 6 equal balls, then **ROLL** each ball into 6-inch-long sausages.

2. PLACE sausages on a foil-lined baking sheet, cover with plastic wrap, and **REFRIGERATE** for 2 hours or overnight.

3. BRUSH or spray the grill grid with vegetable oil. **PREHEAT** grill to medium-high.

4. GRILL sausages with lid lowered for 10 minutes, turning often so they cook evenly. **REMOVE** from grill and place on a plate, covering with aluminum foil to keep warm.

5. GRILL pita rounds 1 minute per side or until just warmed.

6. SPREAD hummus over one side of pita and place sausage in center. **FOLD** pita over sausage and **SERVE** immediately.

TIPS AND TECHNIQUES

Ask the Experts

What is allspice?

No, it's not a mix of spices. Allspice is a spice unto itself—the pea-size berry of the evergreen pimento tree, a native of the West Indies and South America. Available either ground or whole, the dried berries have a taste that calls to mind nutmeg, cinnamon, and cloves—hence the name. It is also sometimes called Jamaica pepper.

Tasty Hummus

Pureed chickpeas are the main ingredient of hummus, a smooth Middle Eastern paste flavored with garlic, lemon juice, and either olive or sesame oil. Usually served as a dip with pita bread, fresh hummus is readily available in the refrigerated-foods section of your supermarket.

Don't be surprised when you find hummus in every flavor under the sun—lemon, garlic, roasted red pepper, and olive, among others. One may go well in a sandwich and another may not, depending on the sandwich's other ingredients and seasonings. To be on the safe side, try a flavored hummus as a dip before making it part of a sandwich.

It also pays to try different brands of hummus, which vary widely in taste and quality. And remember that high-priced doesn't always mean better.

The perfect solution to leftover chicken—great as an appetizer or as a light lunch or supper

GRILLED CHICKEN AND MUSHROOM QUESADILLAS

Serves 12–16 ◆◆ Prep Time: 15 minutes ◆◆ Grilling Time: 6 minutes; medium heat

INGREDIENTS

¼ cup butter (half a stick)

1 tablespoon vegetable oil

4 cloves garlic, minced

8 ounces fresh mushrooms (such as shiitake, button, or cremini), stemmed and sliced

5 scallions, chopped

1 tablespoon dried thyme

1¾ cups shredded cooked chicken

1 tablespoon lime juice

½ cup chopped fresh cilantro (or flat-leaf parsley)

2¾ cups grated Monterey Jack cheese

Salt and pepper to taste

16 5½-inch flour tortillas

Olive oil for coating

1. MELT the butter with the vegetable oil in a large skillet over medium heat. Add garlic and **SAUTE** for 1 minute. Add mushrooms, scallions, and thyme, and sauté until tender, about 10 minutes.

2. REMOVE skillet from heat and **STIR** in chicken, lime juice, and cilantro. Then stir in cheese and **SEASON** with salt and pepper. Cover and **REFRIGERATE** until ready to use (the mixture can be prepared as long as 8 hours in advance).

3. PREHEAT grill to medium. **BRUSH** one side of each tortilla with olive oil.

4. PLACE 8 tortillas, oiled-side down, on 2 baking sheets. **SPREAD** chicken mixture evenly on tortillas and **TOP** with another tortilla, oiled-side up. To flatten each tortilla sandwich, **PRESS** with a large metal spatula.

5. TRANSFER the tortillas to the grill and **GRILL** for 3 minutes on each side or until golden brown. Remove from grill, let rest for 1 minute, then **CUT** into wedges with a pizza wheel or large knife. **SERVE** warm.

Chicken and Mushroom Tostada

You can use the ingredients in this quesadilla recipe to make a tostada—a fried corn tortilla topped or filled with a mixture of ingredients.

Using 8 tortillas (remember that tostadas call for the *corn*, not flour, kind), heat 1/2 inch of veg-etable oil in a skillet over medium-high heat, and fry each tortilla for about 2 minutes or until the bubbling stops and the tortilla is crisp.

Top each tortilla with the sautéed mushroom mixture, then the chicken, shredded lettuce, chopped tomatoes, and shredded cheese.

Ask the Experts

How tricky is it to grill quesadillas?

Not very, once you've practiced. The key to grilling these piquant Mexican delights is to cook them so that the cheese melts but the tortillas don't burn. As with pizza, it's smart to have a cooler safety zone on the grill where you can move a quesadilla if it starts to char too quickly.

Another tip: You can stuff quesadillas with just about anything your heart desires—from vegetables to beef to seafood to chicken. The possibilities are endless, so have some fun!

Red and yellow bell peppers add color to this pizza,
made with your choice of kielbasa or Italian sausage

PESTO PIZZA WITH SAUSAGE AND PEPPERS

Serves 4–8 ↦ Prep Time: 15–20 minutes ↦ Grilling Time: 19–20 minutes; medium heat

INGREDIENTS

4 bags prepared pizza dough

1 pound kielbasa or hot Italian sausages, cut into 1/2-inch slices

1 large red bell pepper, cored, seeded, and cut into 1/4-inch strips

1 large yellow bell pepper, cored, seeded, and cut into 1/4-inch strips

2 medium red onions, peeled and cut into eighths

3/4 cup olive oil

1/3 cup balsamic vinegar

6 cloves garlic, minced

3 teaspoons dried mixed herbs such as rosemary, basil, and thyme

16 ounces prepared pesto (or see recipe on page 117)

2 cups grated mozzarella cheese

2/3 cup grated Parmesan cheese

2 cups crumbled goat cheese

1. **BRUSH** or spray grill grid with vegetable oil.

2. **PREHEAT** the grill to medium.

3. **SLIDE** or drape pizza dough onto the grill. **GRILL** for 2 to 3 minutes or until you see the dough puff and the underside is crisp.

4. Using tongs, **REMOVE** dough from grill and place on work surface, grilled-side up.

5. **ARRANGE** sausage, peppers, and onions in a large roasting pan. **WHISK** together the olive oil, vinegar, garlic, and herbs. **POUR** over vegetables and **TOSS** to coat.

6. **TRANSFER** vegetables and sausage to a perforated grill pan (see page 76) and **GRILL** for about 12 minutes, turning occasionally, until slightly charred. **REMOVE** from grill.

7. When ready to assemble, **SPREAD** an equal amount of Pesto over well-grilled side of each crust. **SPRINKLE** each round with an equal amount of mozzarella and Parmesan cheese. **ADD** sausages, peppers, and onions, and top with a sprinkling of goat cheese.

8. Using a large spatula, **RETURN** pizzas to grill. **CLOSE** grill lid and **GRILL** pizzas for about 5 minutes or until hot and bubbly (rotate the pizzas during cooking).

9. **REMOVE** pizzas from grill, let rest for 1 minute, and **CUT** into slices. **SERVE** immediately.

Ask the Experts

How different is kielbasa from Italian sausage?
A smoked Polish sausage, **kielbasa** is most often made from pork, although either beef or turkey is sometimes added. Its links are usually sold precooked. Italian sausage, also made from pork, comes uncooked and must be grilled, fried, or braised. **Sweet Italian sausage** is flavored with garlic and fennel, while **hot Italian sausage** gets its heat from hot red pepper.

Where can I purchase prepared pizza dough?
You can find fresh pizza dough in 15-ounce bags in the dairy section of most supermarkets. Refrigerate until ready to use.

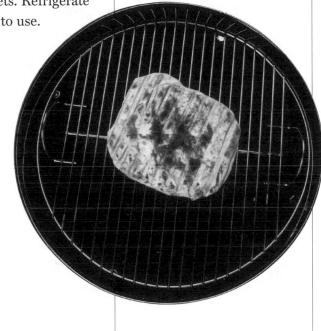

*This is the simplest of all pizzas—
and so easy to make on the grill*

PIZZA MARGHERITA

Makes 4 8-inch pizzas (usually 1 to 2 servings per pizza)
Prep Time: 15–20 minutes ⇥ Grilling Time: 16 minutes; medium heat

INGREDIENTS

4 bags prepared pizza dough

$\frac{1}{3}$ to $\frac{1}{2}$ cup olive oil

8 cloves garlic, minced

1 teaspoon each salt and pepper

12 ounces mozzarella cheese, thinly sliced

8 plum tomatoes, cored, cut into $\frac{1}{2}$-inch slices

8 tablespoons grated Parmesan cheese

1 tablespoon dried basil; or 24 basil leaves, whole or chopped

1. BRUSH or spray the grill grid with vegetable oil. **PREHEAT** grill to medium.

2. SLIDE one pizza dough onto grill and cook about 3 minutes or until the top of the dough puffs and the underside crisps. **TURN** dough over with tongs, **BRUSH** top of pizza dough with oil, and continue to cook another minute.

3. REMOVE dough from grill with tongs and place on work surface, well-grilled side up. **REPEAT** with all dough rounds.

4. SPRINKLE each of the pizzas with a little garlic, salt, and pepper.

5. DIVIDE the mozzarella and tomato slices evenly among the pizzas. **SPRINKLE** each with 2 tablespoons Parmesan cheese, **ADD** the basil, and return the rounds to the grill.

6. COVER the grill and **COOK** for an additional 1 to 2 minutes, being careful not to burn the dough (if dough becomes too browned, move to a cooler part of the grill). When bottom crust is browned and firm, **REMOVE** pizza from grill with a large metal spatula. **CUT** into quarters and **SERVE**.

Pizza Margherita originated in Naples, or so the
legend goes. The three colors—red, white, and green—
represent the colors of the Italian flag.

These Italian sandwiches make great appetizers when cut into quarters

GRILLED GOAT CHEESE AND TOMATO PANINI

Serves 10 ↔ Prep Time: 30 minutes ↔ Grilling Time: 2–4 minutes; low heat

INGREDIENTS

20 slices firm white sandwich bread

Olive oil for brushing bread

4 6-ounce logs fresh goat cheese, room temperature

1 cup prepared or home-made pesto (see recipe on page 117)

8 medium plum toma-toes, sliced into ¼-inch-thick rounds

1. BRUSH one side of each slice of bread with olive oil and place on a work surface, oiled-side down.

2. On each slice of bread, **PLACE** ½ ounce goat cheese, 1 tablespoon pesto, 4 slices tomato, and another ½ ounce goat cheese, then **TOP** with another bread slice, oiled-side up.

3. BRUSH or spray the grill grid with vegetable oil. **PREHEAT** grill to low.

4. PLACE sandwiches on perforated grill pan (see page 76) over heat and **WEIGH** them down with a heavy iron skillet. **GRILL** for 1 to 2 minutes on each side or until they are crisp and very brown.

5. REMOVE panini from grill, **CUT** into halves or quarters on the diagonal, and **SERVE** hot.

TIPS AND TECHNIQUES

Ask the Experts

What is panini?

Panini is simply the plural of *panino*, the Italian word for bread or roll. In the United States, the word has come to mean a pressed or flattened sandwich of meats, vegetables, and/or cheese.

Tomatoes for Cooking

This recipe uses plum tomatoes for good reason: Their relatively dry flesh won't leak and make the bread soggy. In fact, plum tomatoes have traditionally been used for cooking and canning, not for eating fresh. First developed in Italy in the midnineteenth century, they have firm flesh with few seeds and little gel, which means they will cook down to a thick paste or sauce. And like meaty beefsteak tomatoes, they are good for grilling.

Think twice before replacing plum with cherry tomatoes in a recipe. The cherry tomato's thin skin and copious gel often lead to disappointing results.

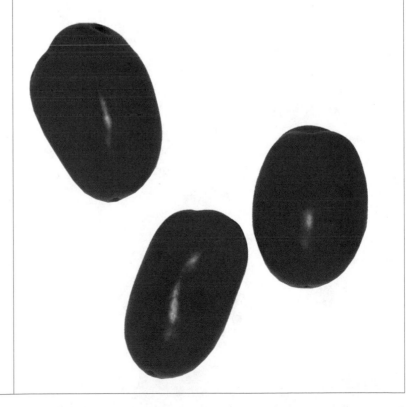

You can use any mild-tasting, firm-fleshed fish fillet in these sandwiches

GRILLED MAHIMAHI SANDWICHES

Serves 6 ↦ Prep Time: 20 minutes ↦ Grilling Time: 12–14 minutes; medium heat

INGREDIENTS

3 tablespoons olive oil

3 cloves garlic, minced

1½ tablespoons chili powder

½ teaspoon pepper

6 6-ounce mahimahi or sea bass fillets, skin removed, each about 1-inch thick

12 slices French or sourdough bread, sliced ½ inch thick

Olive oil for brushing bread

1 cup Lime Mayonnaise (see recipe on opposite page)

12 tomato slices

Lettuce leaves

1. In a small bowl, **WHISK** together the olive oil, garlic, chili powder, and pepper. **BRUSH** mixture on both sides of the fish and **PLACE** on a platter.

2. BRUSH or spray the grill grid with vegetable oil. **PREHEAT** grill to medium.

3. PLACE fish fillets on grill and **COOK** for 5 minutes on each side or until just opaque. During the last few minutes of grilling, **BRUSH** bread with a small amount of olive oil and grill about 1 to 2 minutes on each side or until lightly browned.

4. REMOVE fish and bread from grill and **SPREAD** Lime Mayonnaise on one side of each bread slice. **PLACE** one fish fillet on each of 6 pieces of bread and **TOP** with tomato and lettuce. Place a slice of bread on top, then **SERVE** warm.

TIPS AND TECHNIQUES

Lime Mayonnaise

3/4 cup mayonnaise

2/3 cup finely chopped leeks (white and pale-green parts)

3 tablespoons lime juice

1 teaspoon chili powder

2 cloves garlic, minced

1. In a small mixing bowl, **COMBINE** the mayonnaise, leeks, lime juice, chili powder, and garlic.

2. Cover and **CHILL** until ready to use.

Ask the Experts

What other kinds of fish can I use in this recipe?

Halibut, turbot, and orange roughy will stand up to the strong flavor of the chili-powder–flavored sauce.

What are leeks?

Leeks are relatives of onions with a sweet, mild oniony flavor that works well in soups, potato dishes, and stews. They look a bit like large green onions. You want young, tender leeks that are about 1 inch in diameter and about 9 to 12 inches long. Their stalks may be full of dirt, so be sure to wash them thoroughly.

To clean leeks, trim off the rough ends of the dark green leaves and discard. Make a slit down the center and pull the leek apart. Wash each half thoroughly under cold water, bending them back to rinse away every bit of grit hidden between the layers. Pat dry with paper towels.

A Fish Renamed

Inhabiting tropical and semitropical seas, mahi-mahi was once known as dolphin fish even though it bears no resemblance to the frisky marine mammal. Its modern, more musical name dates from ancient Hawaii, where its firm and flavorful flesh has made mahimahi a favorite in restaurants.

The combination of flavors in this sandwich calls
to mind spanakopita, the Greek spinach pie

SPINACH AND FETA TORTILLAS

Serves 6 (makes 4 10-inch rounds) ⇥ Prep Time: 15 minutes
Grilling Time: 4–6 minutes; medium heat

INGREDIENTS

2½ tablespoons olive oil

8 cloves garlic, chopped

2 10-ounce boxes frozen-leaf spinach, thawed and squeezed dry

8 medium plum tomatoes, coarsely chopped

1 tablespoon mixed dried herbs; or 3 tablespoons chopped fresh herbs, such as oregano, basil, thyme, and rosemary

3 tablespoons olive oil

1 tablespoon balsamic vinegar

¼ teaspoon each salt and pepper

3 green onions, white and green parts

6 ounces crumbled feta cheese

4 10-inch flour tortillas

1. HEAT oil in a medium skillet over medium heat. **ADD** the garlic and spinach and **SAUTÉ** for 2 minutes or until spinach is slightly wilted. Set aside.

2. In a medium bowl, **COMBINE** the tomatoes, herbs, olive oil, vinegar, salt, and pepper. Set aside.

3. BRUSH or spray the grill grid with vegetable oil. **PREHEAT** grill to medium.

4. BRUSH one side of each tortilla with olive oil and place on grill, oiled-side down, for 1 minute or until tortilla starts to puff. Remove with tongs and **BRUSH** ungrilled side with oil.

5. Set tortillas on work surface, grilled-side up. Evenly distribute spinach and tomatoes on each tortilla. **SPRINKLE** with equal amounts green onions and feta cheese.

6. FOLD each tortilla in half and press down with your hands.

7. Using a large spatula, **TRANSFER** the folded tortillas to the grill, close the lid, and **COOK** for 2 to 3 minutes, rotating tortillas for even cooking. (Move tortillas to a cooler part of the grill if they start to char before the feta cheese has melted.) **REMOVE** tortillas from grill and **SLICE** into wedges. **SERVE**.

The Mediterranean meets Mexico in this tasty sandwich.
The spinach and feta cheese of the Greek specialty spanakopita are
grilled between flour tortillas instead of phyllo dough.

Flank steak should marinate overnight if
possible, so plan accordingly

FLANK STEAK SANDWICHES WITH HORSERADISH SAUCE

Serves 6 ⇥ Prep Time: 15 minutes ⇥ Marinating Time: at least 8 hours
Grilling Time: 15 minutes; high heat

INGREDIENTS

1 1- to 2-pound flank
steak

2 tablespoons Dijon-style
mustard

1/3 cup dry red wine

1/4 cup olive oil

2 cloves garlic, minced

1 teaspoon dried rosemary or 1 tablespoon
chopped fresh rosemary

1/2 teaspoon pepper

6 focaccia or long French
bread rolls; or 2 French
bread loaves cut into
thirds, then cut in half
lengthwise

3/4 cup prepared or
Homemade Horseradish
Sauce (see recipe on
opposite page)

1/2 pound sliced fontina
or Swiss cheese

Lettuce leaves, optional

1. BRUSH both sides of flank steak with mustard. In a small bowl, **COMBINE** the red wine, olive oil, garlic, rosemary, and pepper. Place steak in a large resealable plastic bag, **POUR** in the mixture, seal the bag, and **MARINATE** in the refrigerator for at least 8 hours or overnight.

2. REMOVE flank steak from bag, discarding the marinade.

3. BRUSH or spray the grill grid with vegetable oil. **PREHEAT** grill to high.

4. GRILL steak with lid down for 7 to 8 minutes on each side for medium-rare. Remove steak to a cutting board and let **REST** for 5 minutes. **SLICE** steak thinly, across the grain, on a diagonal.

5. Lightly **GRILL** focaccia 30 seconds or until golden. **SPREAD** a small amount of horseradish on one side of bread, **TOP** with steak, one slice of cheese, and a lettuce leaf. Cover with another slice of bread. **CUT** sandwiches in half and **SERVE** warm. Or wrap in foil, refrigerate, and serve chilled.

TIPS AND TECHNIQUES

Horseradish Root

If you use fresh horseradish root for a sauce, wear rubber gloves to scrub the root and peel the skin. Also, be careful not to rub your eyes.

Grate the root with a cheese grater and combine with mayonnaise or sour cream and the seasonings of your choice. Grate about an inch of the stalk for each $3/4$ cup of sauce, and taste for hotness as you add.

Homemade Horseradish Sauce

$1/2$ cup mayonnaise

2 tablespoons Dijon-style mustard

2 teaspoons prepared horseradish

1 teaspoon dried chives or 1 tablespoon chopped fresh chives

1 teaspoon lemon juice

Salt and pepper to taste

1. In a small mixing bowl, **COMBINE** the mayonnaise, mustard, horseradish, chives, lemon juice, salt, and pepper. **BLEND** well.

2. Cover and **CHILL** until ready to use.

What is Focaccia?

Focaccia is flat, rather puffy Italian bread that tastes best when liberally brushed with olive oil and sprinkled with salt before it's baked—the source of its marvelous flavor. Fresh rosemary, sage, or thyme is also sometimes pressed into the dough.

The focaccia sold in supermarkets is often topped with sliced tomatoes, onions, or other vegetables or herbs, much like a pizza.

Brimming with vegetables and herbs, this
sandwich has the taste of the South of France

GRILLED VEGETABLE SANDWICHES

Serves 6 ◆▸ Prep Time: 20–25 minutes ◆▸ Grilling Time: 15 minutes; medium-high heat

INGREDIENTS

3 large red bell peppers,
cored, seeded, and
quartered

3 medium zucchinis, sliced
lengthwise 1/4-inch thick

6 large portobello mushrooms, stemmed

6 1/2-inch-thick-rounds of
eggplant

1 large red onion, cut into
1/4-inch-thick slices

3 large tomatoes, cut into
12 1/4-inch-thick slices

6 Italian or French bread
rolls

3/4 cup olive oil

2 teaspoons dried thyme
or 2 tablespoons chopped
fresh thyme

4 cloves garlic, minced

1/4 cup balsamic vinegar

Salt and pepper to taste

12 thin slices provolone or
fontina cheese

2/3 cup chopped fresh basil

I. PREHEAT grill to medium-high.

2. ARRANGE vegetables in a large glass or ceramic dish. **SPLIT**
the Italian bread rolls lengthwise.

3. In a medium bowl, **WHISK** together the olive oil, thyme, garlic, vinegar, salt, and pepper. **BRUSH** both sides of the rolls with
the marinade mixture. **POUR** remaining marinade over the
vegetables, then **TOSS** to coat thoroughly.

4. GRILL cut sides of rolls about 1 to 2 minutes or until toasted.

5. GRILL vegetables in a perforated grill pan for 12 to 14 minutes or until tender and slightly charred, turning and brushing
with marinade several times during grilling.

6. ARRANGE grilled vegetables on bottom of each of 6 rolls and
TOP with 2 slices of cheese, a sprinkle of fresh basil, and the top
of the roll. **SERVE** warm.

Ask the Experts

What is meant by "extra-virgin" olive oil?

Olive oils vary in color, flavor, and fragrance, and they're best when cold-pressed, a process that uses only pressure (not chemicals) to extract the oil from the olives.

Olive oils are classified by their degree of acidity, and those with the lowest acidity are the most desirable. Lowest in acidity but highest in flavor and price is **extra-virgin** olive oil. **Virgin** olive oil has a slightly higher acidity level, while **fino** olive oil is a blend of extra-virgin and virgin oils. **Pure** olive oil (no "virgin" in the name) has the most acid and is the least flavorful of all the olive oils.

How long will olive oil keep in my cupboard?

In a cool, dark place, olive oil will last up to 6 months. If you keep it in the refrigerator, it will last up to a year. Olive oil will solidify in the fridge, so take it out and bring it to room temperature before using.

GLOSSARY

AL DENTE Slightly underdone with a chewy consistency. Italian for "to the tooth." The term is usually applied to the cooking of pasta but may also be used to describe vegetables that are not fully cooked.

BAKE To cook by free-circulating dry air in an enclosed space, such as an oven. Baking usually refers to cakes, cookies, pies, etc., as opposed to roasting, which refers to meat.

BARBECUE Technically, to cook meat using indirect heat in an enclosed space over natural woods. However, "barbecue" and "grill" have become synonymous, both meaning to cook food directly over intense heat, usually out of doors using natural woods, charcoal, or gas, on a grill, in an open pit, or on a spit.

BASTE To pour, brush, or drizzle a liquid over whatever it is you are cooking in order to moisten it and add flavor. A bulb baster makes basting easy.

BEAT To blend or mix ingredients rapidly so that air is incorporated, resulting in a smooth, creamy mixture of greater volume.

BLANCH To plunge food briefly into boiling water in order to tenderize it or mellow its flavor. Blanching also enhances the color of vegetables.

BLEND To combine ingredients to a desired consistency.

BOIL To heat water or other liquids to 212°F (at sea level); bubbles will form and rise.

BONE To remove the bones from meat, poultry, fish, or game. A boning knife is a handy tool for such chores.

BRAISE To cook meat or vegetables in a small amount of liquid in a tightly closed container. This method is ideal for tougher cuts of meat, firm-fleshed fish, and numerous vegetables.

BREAD To dredge or coat food with breadcrumbs.

BROIL To cook with intense heat, usually by placing under the broiling heat element of an oven. (In most ovens, the broiling heat element is on the top, the baking heat element on the bottom.) The high heat seals in juices, allowing a food's outside to brown but keeping the inside tender.

BROWN To cook briefly in hot fat, allowing a crust (usually brown) to form on all sides and sealing in the juices. This method also enriches the flavor of the food.

CHARCOAL There are several different types of charcoal. **Charwood**, also known as lump charcoal or chunk charwood, is charcoal made by burning whole logs or large pieces of wood in a kiln without oxygen. This type of charcoal is pure and burns very hot. **Natural briquettes** are made from pulverized wood held together with natural starches. **Composition briquettes** are made from wood scraps and/or coal dust that is bound by paraffin or petroleum. Briquettes do not burn cleanly.

CHIMNEY STARTER Aids in igniting charcoal fire. A simple device that is usually six to eight inches in diameter with vent holes at the bottom and a grate in the middle on which to place the charcoal. Newspaper or a paraffin starter is placed in the bottom section, and the device is set on the charcoal grate in the grill and lit. Chimney starters have heat-proof handles and are favored by grill buffs.

CHOP To use a knife to cut up food into small uniform pieces or cubes.

CLARIFY To separate the clear, liquid part of a mixture from the solids.

CUT or **CUT IN** A pastry term meaning to mix shortening or butter with flour or other dry ingredients until the mixture resembles coarse meal. To do this, you can use two knives and cut the shortening or butter directly into the flour, or use your fingers to mix it into the flour.

DASH A very small quantity; a scant ⅛ of a teaspoon.

DEGLAZE To create a sauce from the little bits of meat or poultry left in a pan after browning, sautéing, broiling, or roasting, by adding a small amount of liquid, mixing it all together, and allowing it to boil up.

DEVEIN To use a sharp knife or special deveining tool to remove the dark vein that runs along the back of a shrimp.

DICE To cut food into small, equal-size cubes, usually ranging in size from ⅛ to ¼ inch.

DREDGE To lightly coat food, usually with flour, cornmeal, or breadcrumbs. One quick method is to place the coating material in a zip-top bag, add the food to be coated, then seal the bag and shake.

DRIP PANS Placed under the grill grate, aluminum foil drip pans are essential for catching fat. Also used to soak wood chips and to keep grilled foods warm next to the grill. Available at grocery stores.

ELECTRIC STARTER This features a metal loop that heats up when the starter is plugged in. When using, bury the loop beneath the mound of charcoal, then plug in the starter. When the coals at the core of the mound are red hot, unplug and remove the starter. Make sure to place it on a non-flammable surface and let it cool.

FLAKE To test the flesh of a fish to see if it is done by using a fork to break away a small piece or flake.

FOLD To gently incorporate one ingredient into another, not by stirring or beating but by lifting from underneath with a rubber spatula.

FRY To cook food in hot fat in a skillet until brown and crisp.

GARNISH To decorate foods with fresh herbs, edible flowers, fresh vegetables, nuts, or fruit, to enhance the appearance of the dish.

GAS GRILL An American invention consisting of a metal box lined with tube-shaped liquid propane burners. The burners lie underneath heating surfaces—usually ceramic briquettes or V-shaped metal bars. Most gas grills have a minimum of two heating zones.

GRATE To rub a food against a rough surface (such as the side of a grater) to get fine shreds or tiny chunks. Used with cheeses and vegetables.

GREASE To lightly coat a pan with a bit of butter, oil, or vegetable oil cooking spray to prevent cooked food from sticking.

GRILL To cook food directly over intense heat on a rack over hot coals, natural wood, or gas. See BARBECUE and INDIRECT GRILLING.

HIBACHI A small, portable charcoal grill originating in Japan and designed for direct high-heat grilling of kebabs, satays, and small cuts of meat, poultry, seafood, or vegetables.

INDIRECT GRILLING To cook food by placing it on the unlit portion of the grill and closing the lid. This method cooks food without charring it.

JULIENNE To cut fresh vegetables or other foods into thin, matchstick-size pieces of the same length.

KEBAB Sometimes spelled kabab, Turkish for "broiled meat." Shish kebab is skewered broiled meat, usually lamb. Nowadays, kebab applies to any small piece of food that is grilled on a skewer, such as cut vegetables, poultry, fish, or meat.

KETTLE GRILL Uniquely American, this has a deep, rounded bowl with a grate in the bottom for holding charcoal or chunks of wood and a grate on the top for food. The grill top is also bowl-shaped, allowing you to turn the grill into an outdoor oven or smoker. Cooking temperature is controlled by vents in the lid and on the bottom.

KNEAD To work a finished dough until it is smooth and elastic. To use the palms of your hands on a lightly floured wooden or marbled bread board.

MARINATE To enhance the flavor and tenderize the texture of a food by placing it in a seasoned liquid, usually a combination of oil, spices, and some type of acidic liquid such as vinegar, juice, or wine.

MELT To dissolve a solid or semisolid over slow heat. The term is most commonly associated with butter and chocolate.

MINCE To cut a food into very fine pieces, not larger than a 1/8-inch square.

MIX To use a spoon or a fork to blend ingredients.

PARBOIL To partially cook food in boiling water or broth. Parboiling is similar to blanching, except the food is left in for a longer period of time when parboiling.

POACH To cook food in a simmering liquid that does not boil. Poaching brings out the full, delicate flavor of a food.

POUND To use a heavy mallet or frying pan to flatten meat or poultry, often between sheets of waxed paper. Pounding helps tenderize meat and poultry.

PREHEAT On gas grills, this means setting to a certain temperature 15 to 20 minutes prior to cooking. With charcoal grills, it means lighting coals 15 to 20 minutes before grilling.

PUREE To use a blender or food processor to turn cooked food into a smooth liquid, which is also called a puree.

REDUCE To boil a sauce to reduce its volume and intensify its flavor.

RENDER To liquefy or leach out the solid fat of a food by heating. It's usually done when cooking meat or poultry.

REST To allow beef, steak, chicken—almost anything you grill—to stand for a few minutes before serving. This allows meat juices, driven to the center of the cut by the searing heat, to return to the surface, resulting in a juicier, more flavorful piece of meat.

ROAST To cook food, usually uncovered, in an enclosed space by the free circulation of dry heat.

SAUTÉ To cook food quickly in a small amount of butter or fat over medium to high heat while turning the food frequently so that it doesn't burn.

SEAR To brown the surface, usually of meat, by a brief exposure to high heat.

SHRED To cut or tear a food into thin strips.

SIMMER To cook food, usually a soup or stew, over low heat so that it almost but never quite reaches a boil. Small bubbles will appear on the surface.

SKEWER A long, needlelike device used to thread pieces of meat, poultry, seafood, or vegetables for grilling. Barbecue skewers come in an array of sizes and shapes—from simple metal skewers, to two-pronged skewers, flat metal skewers, and slender bamboo skewers—each designed for a specific function.

SNIP To use scissors or kitchen shears to cut herbs into small bits.

STEAM To cook food in a covered container using a small amount of boiling liquid.

STEW To cook food slowly over relatively low heat.

STIR To use a spoon or other implement to mix or blend ingredients together in a circular motion, or, if over heat, to move food around to prevent it from burning.

STRAIN To remove solids from liquids by pouring through a sieve, strainer, or colander.

STUFF To fill a cavity with a mixture; for example, poultry, fish, meat, vegetables.

TOAST To brown food by baking it directly under or over heat.

TONGS The most essential tools in a griller's pantry, they enable you to turn meat without stabbing it. When purchasing, look for long, stiff spring-loaded tongs.

TOSS To gently mix food by using a large spoon or fork to lift it from the bottom.

VEGETABLE AND FISH GRIDS A perforated or metal-wire plate placed on top of the grill grate to hold small pieces of food that might fall through. Also good for fragile foods like fish fillets.

WHIP To rapidly beat a food such as cream, either by hand by using a fork or whisk, or with an electric mixer or food processor. Whipping adds a great deal of air, thereby increasing the food's volume.

WHISK To mix sauces, dressings, eggs, or other liquids in a swift, circular motion, usually using a balloon-shaped wire instrument also called a whisk.

INDEX

THE AUTHOR: UP CLOSE

Pamela Richards is a professional chef and cooking instructor and the author of **I'm in the Kitchen, Now What?!** She enjoys teaching cooking to beginning students. "The trick is to explain the rules of cooking without dampening the fun." Her favorite classes to teach are those using the grill. That's because grilling is not simply a pastime to her, but a passion. In **I've got a Grill, Now What?!** Pam's enthusiasm comes shining through. As she tells her first-time grilling students: "Relax and enjoy the experience!" Pam lives in Allendale, New Jersey, with her two daughters.

Barbara J. Morgan Publisher, Silver Lining Books

I've got a Grill, Now What?! ™

Barb Chintz Editorial Director

Leonard Vigliarolo Design Director

Hilary Davis Tonken Editor

Fred DuBose Contributing Writer

Della R. Mancuso Production Manager

Marguerite Daniels Editorial Assistant